First Lessons®

Folk Guitar Method

by Corey Christiansen

Online Audio & Video

Audio
www.melbay.com/99919BCDEB

Video
dv.melbay.com/99919

You Tube
www.melbay.com/99919V

AUDIO CONTENTS

1 Tuning [1:22]
2 Exercise #1 [:33]
3 Exercise #2 [:33]
4 Exercise #3 [:27]
5 Exercise #4 [:26]
6 Aura Lee [:51]
7 Amazing Grace [:44]
8 Exercise #8 [:23]
9 Exercise #9 [:22]
10 Exercise #10 [:21]
11 Down Up Strumming Exercise [:33]
12 She'll Be Comin' Round the Mountain [:47]
13 Streets of Laredo [:39]
14 Notes on the First String [:32]
15 Notes on the Second String [:30]
16 Folks Wagon [:28]
17 Notes on the Third String [:22]
18 Red River Valley [:49]
19 Notes on the Fourth String [:26]
20 Notes on the Fifth String [:31]
21 Notes on the Sixth String [:26]
22 Oh Susana [:49]
23 When the Saints Go Marching In [:36]
24 Alternating Bass #1 [:36]
25 Alternating Bass #2 [:31]
26 Kum Ba Yah [:44]
27 Down in the Valley [:36]
28 Going Down the Road Feeling Bad [:45]
29 Fingerstyle Accompaniment #1 [:47]
30 Fingerstyle Accompaniment #2 [:22]
31 Fingerstyle Accompaniment #3 [:24]
32 Fingerstyle Accompaniment #4 [:22]
33 Fingerstyle Accompaniment #5 [:20]
34 Fingerstyle Accompaniment #6 [:20]
35 Fingerstyle Accompaniment #7 [:22]
36 Fingerstyle Accompaniment #8 [:22]
37 Fingerstyle Accompaniment #9 [:20]
38 Fingerstyle Accompaniment #10 [:17]
39 Shenandoah [:45]
40 Scarborough Fair [:40]
41 Worried Man Blues [:41]

MEL BAY® It doesn't get any easier.....

2 3 4 5 6 7 8 9 0

Visit us on the Web at www.melbay.com — E-mail us at email@melbay.com

Table of Contents

Introduction

This beginning guitar method is unique in that it teaches the basics of playing guitar while focusing on the style of folk guitar. Even though this book focuses on one style of guitar playing, it is a beginning method and can used by anyone that has never had a guitar lesson. This method will teach the basics of strumming chords using a variety of styles and techniques. Reading standard notation and tablature in first position will also be presented in a way that is easy to understand.

This book is written so it can be studied from front to back, cover to cover, or by skipping from section to section. For example, one could start with the section on chords and strumming patterns and then skip to the section on reading standard notation. Anyone who practices and learns the exercises and tunes in this book will be able to play simple melodies and accompany themselves and others while singing. Good luck and have fun.

-Corey

Parts of the Guitar

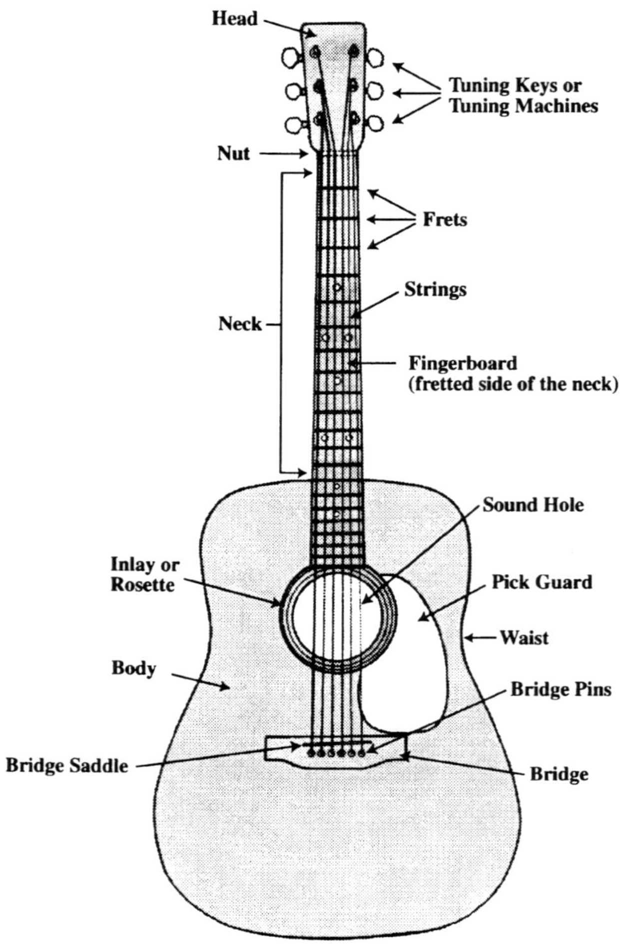

Care of the Guitar

Here are some tips to keep in mind for taking care of the guitar:

1) Make sure the correct type of strings are on the guitar. There are basically two types of strings: nylon and steel. Nylon strings are used on the classical guitar and steel strings are used on the steel string acoustic (folk) guitar and electric guitar (unless the electric has an "acoustic" pick-up). Steel strings which are bronze are for the steel string acoustic guitar. Bronze strings do not work well on electric guitars unless the electric has an "acoustic pick-up". Most guitars play best if they are strung with medium or light gauge strings. Note: heavy gauge strings may warp the neck on some guitars.

2) Avoid rapid temperature and/or humidity changes. A rapid change could damage the finish and the wood of the guitar. Do not leave the guitar in a car when the weather is very hot or cold, and try not to leave the guitar next to heater vents or air conditioners. If the climate is extremely dry, a guitar humidifier can be used to prevent the guitar from drying and cracking.

3) Polish the guitar. Polish which is made specifically for guitars can be purchased from a music store. Besides keeping the guitar looking nice, polishing the guitar will help protect the finish and the woods. Be careful not to polish the fingerboard.

4) If the guitar is being shipped or taken on an airplane, always loosen the strings. The strings do not have to be completely loose, but should be loose enough that the tension of the strings pulling on the neck is greatly reduced.

Holding Position

If the guitar is held properly, it will feel comfortable to you. In the **sitting position,** the guitar is held with the waist of the guitar resting on the right leg. The side of the guitar sits flat on the leg with the neck extending to the left. The neck should be tilted upward slightly so the left arm does not rest on the left leg. Both feet should be flat on the floor, although some guitarists prefer to elevate the right leg by using a footstool. The right arm rests on the top of the guitar just beyond the elbow. The right hand should be placed over and to the back (towards the bridge) of the sound hole. Whether using a pick or the fingers, the right-hand fingers should be bent slightly. The right-hand fingers may touch the top of the guitar, but they should not be stationary. They move when stroking the strings.

Folk or Jazz Position

The left hand should be positioned with the thumb touching the back of the guitar neck. Do not bend the thumb forward. The thumb should be vertical, touching the neck at the knuckle. Do not position the thumb parallel with the neck. The palm of the left hand should not touch the guitar neck. The left wrist may bend *slightly,* but be careful not to exaggerate the bend.

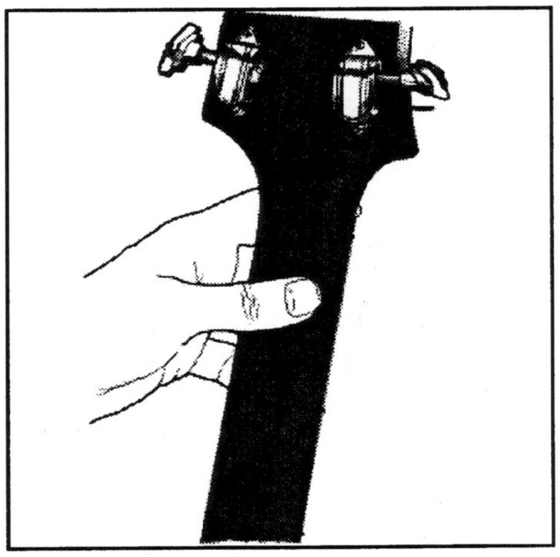

Left-Hand Thumb

When placing a left-hand finger on the string, "square" the finger and push on the string using the tip of the finger. (The fingernails must be short so the tip of the finger can be used.) The finger should be positioned just behind and touching (when possible) the fret wire. Placing the finger too low in the fret may result in a buzz, and placing the finger on top of the fret wire may cause a muted sound. The left-hand knuckles should run parallel with the guitar neck. This makes it possible to reach higher frets with the left-hand third and fourth fingers without turning the wrist. Again, be careful not to bring the left-hand thumb over the top of the guitar neck, and do not touch the guitar neck with the palm of the hand, When pushing on the string, it is as though the guitar neck and string are being pinched between the thumb and finger.

Fingering Notes

Push the string firmly enough to get a sound, but don't over push. To determine the correct amount of pressure, touch the string with the left-hand finger and gradually apply pressure. Pick the string over and over. When a clear sound occurs, that's the amount of pressure to use.

Rest your right-hand thumb on the first (the smallest) string and stroke the open string (open means no left-hand fingers are pushing on the string) downward. Make sure the right-hand wrist moves, and the arm moves slightly from the elbow. The right-hand fingers may touch the top of the guitar, but they should move when the string is played. Try to have a relaxed feeling in the right hand. Go straight down with the thumb when stroking the string. Next, with the right-hand thumb, play the second string open. When playing a string other than the first string, the thumb should go straight down and rest upon (but not play) the next smallest string. In classic guitar playing, this is called a **rest stroke.**

Strumming refers to playing three or more strings so the strings sound simultaneously. To practice the strumming action, rest the right-hand thumb on the fourth string and strum four strings. Using a down stroke, let the right hand fall quickly across the strings so they sound at the same time. The right-hand wrist and arm move with the action.

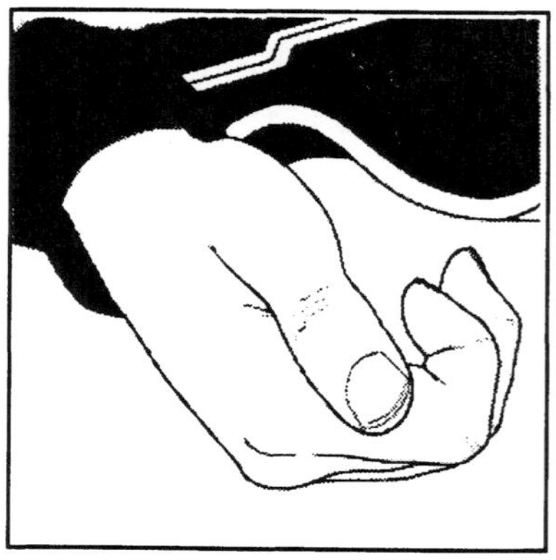

To hold the pick correctly, first, bend the right-hand index finger. The other fingers of the right hand also bend, but not as much as the index finger.

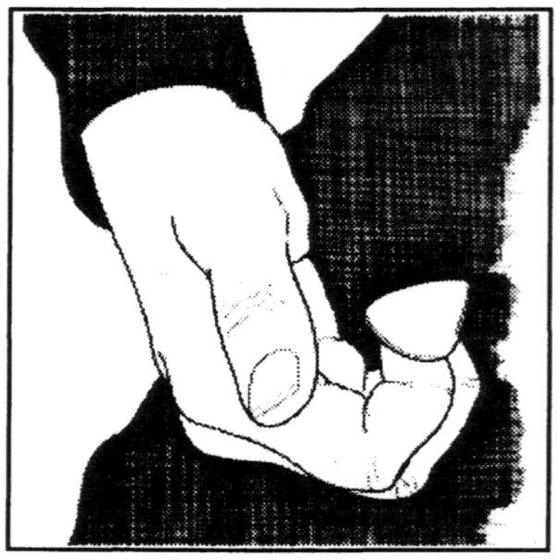

The pick is placed on the end of the index finger with the pointed part of the pick aiming directly at the strings.

The thumb is placed over the pick, covering 2/3 to 3/4 of the pick..

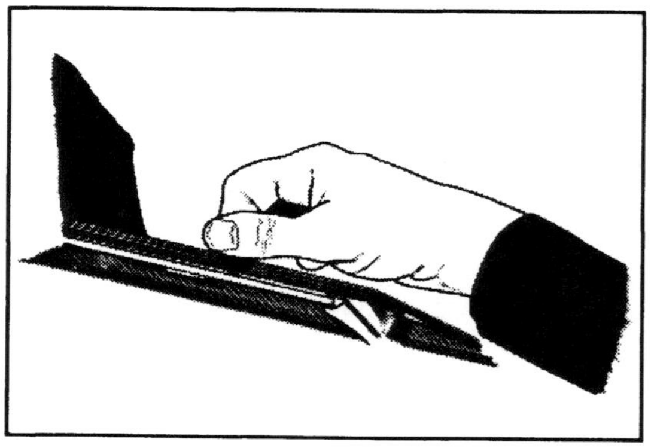

To place the right hand (with the pick) in playing position, rest the pick on the first string. The pick should be tilted upward slightly, rather than at a direct right angle to the string. The pick should stroke the string just over and to the back (towards the bridge) of the sound hole. Pick the first string down. The right-hand wrist should move slightly when the string is played, and the right arm should move slightly from the elbow. When playing strings other than the first, after stroking the string, the pick should rest on the next smallest string. This action is a type of **rest stroke,** which is commonly used in fingerstyle playing, and will generate a richer and fuller tone than picking with an outward motion will. Try playing each of the strings using this type of motion.

To get the feel of strumming with the pick, rest the pick on the fourth string and strum four strings down. Be sure to have a relaxed right hand. Move the wrist and arm slightly when doing the strumming. When picking a single string, or strumming, upward, the pick is tilted down slightly so the pick will glide across the strings, rather than "bite" or snag them.

Fingerstyle

Right Hand

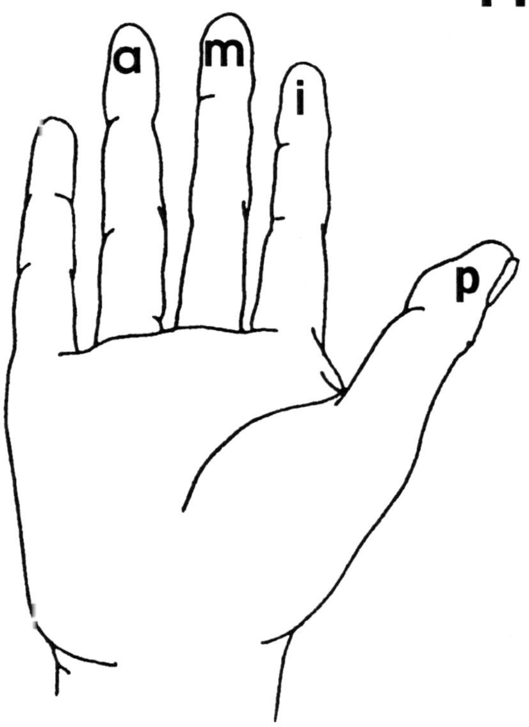

p = pulgar (thumb)
i = índice (index finger)
m = medio (middle finger)
a = anular (ring/third finger)

Playing Two or More Notes Together (Fingerstyle)

Before playing fingerstyle, an understanding of the right-hand position and type of strokes is necessary. Written below are the explanations of the ***rest stroke*** and ***free stroke.***

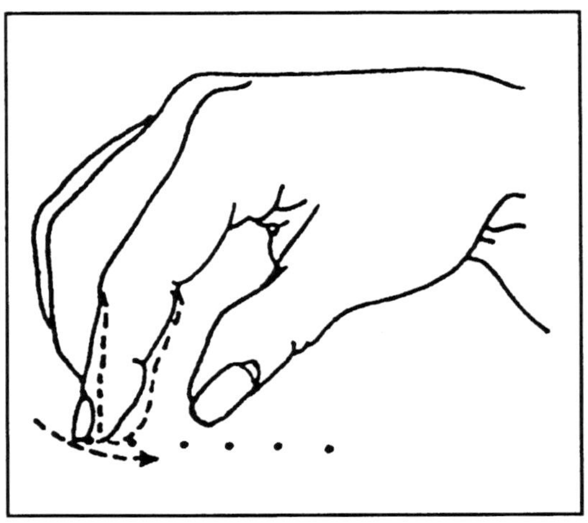

Figure 1

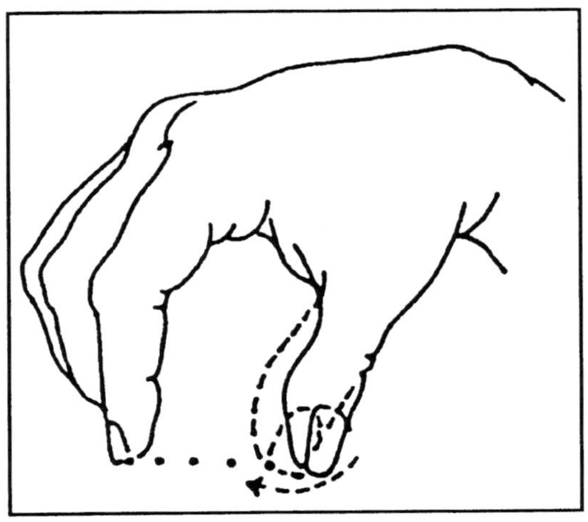

Figure 2

Rest Stroke

The rest stroke is commonly used to play melodies and is popular in solo guitar playing. To do the rest stroke, the flesh on the tip of the finger strokes the string in an upward (not outward) motion. The nail strokes the string as it passes by. *The finger then comes to rest on the next string* (see figure 1).

The thumb rest stroke is done by moving the thumb downward and playing the string with the tip of the thumb and the nail. The thumb then comes to rest on the next string down (see figure 2).

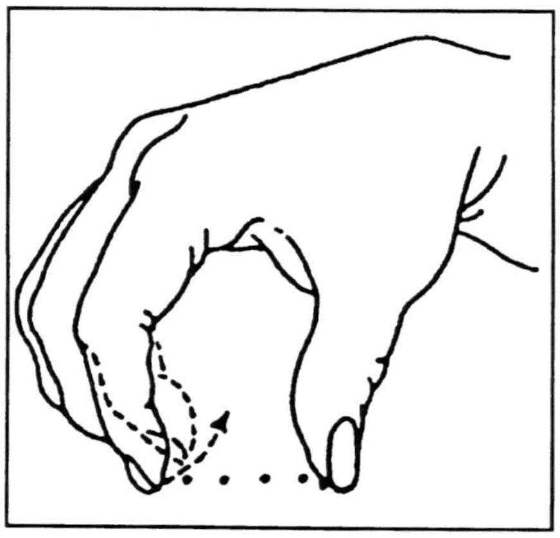

Figure 3

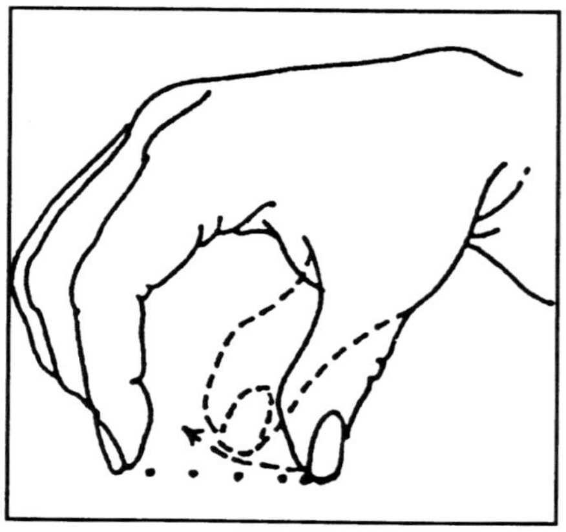

Figure 4

Free Stroke

This is the stroke which is commonly used in accompaniment-style guitar playing. Because it allows the strings to ring, it is good for fingerpicking. It may also be used to play single note melodies. To do the free stroke, the finger picks the string and then is pulled out slightly to *avoid touching the next string.* Remember, it barely misses the next string. Do not pull away from the guitar too far or the string will slap the fretboard (see figure 3).

The free stroke with the thumb is similar to the free stroke with the fingers. After the thumb strikes the string, it is moved slightly outward to avoid hitting the next string (see figure 4).

Playing Two Notes Together

Generally, when music for the guitar is written in two parts, *the thumb plays the notes which have the stems going down and the fingers play the notes with the stems going up.* Each part (the fingers and the thumb) contains the correct number of beats to complete the measure. Therefore, the thumb part may have a rest while the fingers are playing and vice versa.

Tuning

There are several methods which can be used to tune the guitar. One way to tune the guitar is to tune it to itself. You can tune the first string of the guitar to a piano, pitch pipe, tuning fork, or some other instrument, and then match the strings to each other. To do this, use the following steps:

▶ **1.** Tune the first open string to an E note. (Remember, open means that no left-hand fingers are pushing on the string.) You can use a piano, pitch pipe, tuning fork, or another instrument. If you use a tuning fork, use an "E" tuning fork. Hold the fork at the base and tap the fork on your knee, or another object, to get the fork to vibrate. Then, touch the base of the fork near the bottom of the bridge of the guitar. The pitch which will sound is the pitch the first string should have when the string is played open.

▶ **2.** After the first string is tuned, place a left-hand finger on the second string in the fifth fret. Play the first and second strings together. They should be the same pitch. If not, adjust the second string to match the first.

▶ **3.** Place a finger on the third string in the fourth fret. The third string should now sound the same as the second string open. If not, adjust the third string.

▶ **4.** Place a finger on the fourth string in the fifth fret. The fourth string, fifth fret should sound the same as the third string open.

▶ **5.** Place a finger on the fifth string, fifth fret. This should sound the same as the fourth string open.

▶ **6.** Place a finger on the sixth string, fifth fret. The sixth string, fifth fret should sound the same as the fifth string, open.

The diagram below shows where the fingers are placed to tune the guitar to itself.

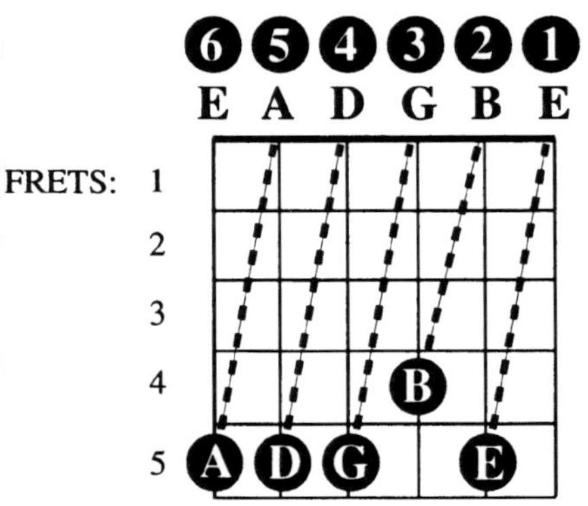

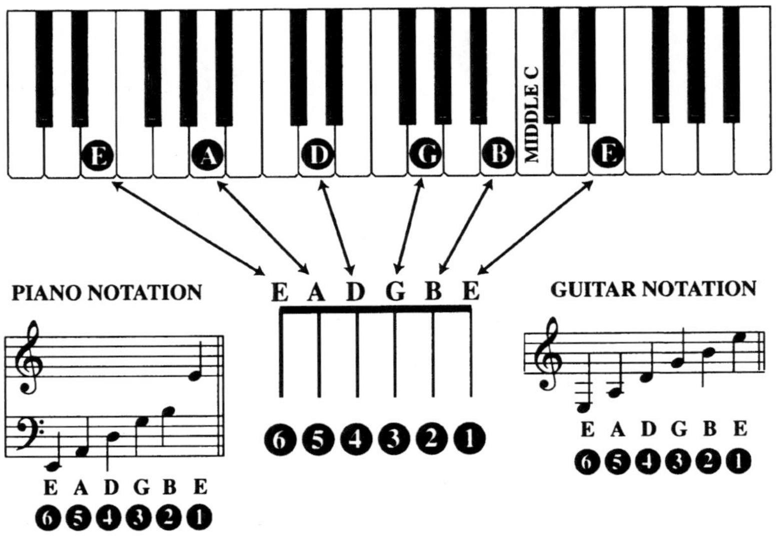

Another common method of tuning makes use of an **electronic tuner**. Tuners utilize lights (LEDs) or VU meters to indicate if a string is sharp or flat. Tuners have built in microphones or electric guitars can be plugged in directly. Follow the instructions provided with the tuner. If the tuner does not respond to playing a string, make sure you are playing the correct string and, if it is adjustable, the tuner is set for that particular string. Sometimes on the lower notes, the tuner won't function properly. If this happens, try playing the harmonic on the twelfth fret of the string. To do this, place a left-hand finger on the string over the twelfth fret-wire. Touch (do not push) the string very lightly. Pick the string. A note should be heard which will have a "chime" effect. This is a harmonic. It will ring longer if the left-hand finger is moved away from the string soon after it is picked. The electronic tuner will most likely respond to this note.

Reading the Music Diagrams

The music in this book will be written using chord diagrams, tablature and standard notation.

Chord diagrams will be used to illustrate chords and scales, With the chord diagrams, the vertical lines represent the strings on the guitar, with the first string being on the right. The horizontal lines represent frets, with the first fret being on the top. Dots, or numbers, on the lines show the placement of left-hand fingers. The numbers on, or next to the dots indicate which left-hand finger to use. A diamond may be used to indicate the placement of the root of the chord or scale. **Root** refers to a note which has the same letter name as the chord or scale.

A zero above a string indicates the string is to be played open (no left-hand fingers are pushing on the string). An "X" above a string indicates that string is not to be played, or that the string is to be muted by tilting one of the left-hand fingers and touching the string lightly.

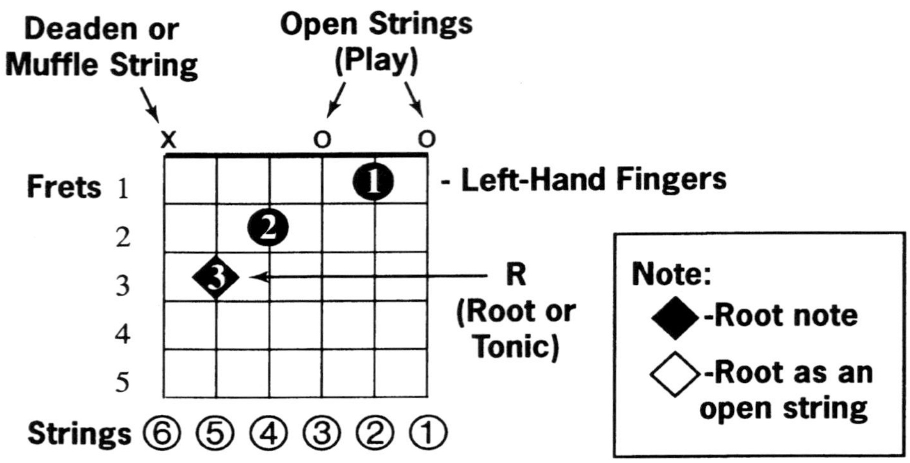

Left-Hand Fingers

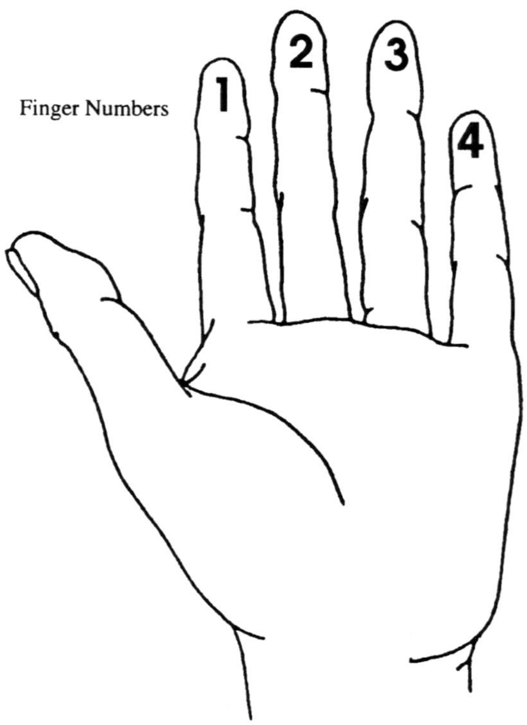

Music Fundamentals

The five lines and four spaces in music is called a **staff**. At the beginning of each line, a treble clef, or G clef, is written on the staff. The treble clef will be discussed later. The staff is divided into sections with **bar lines**. The sections between the bar lines are called **measures**. Inside each measure there are **beats**. Beats are the pulse of the music or measurements of time. The number of beats in each measure can be determined by looking at the **time signature.** The time signature is the fraction which appears at the beginning of the music.

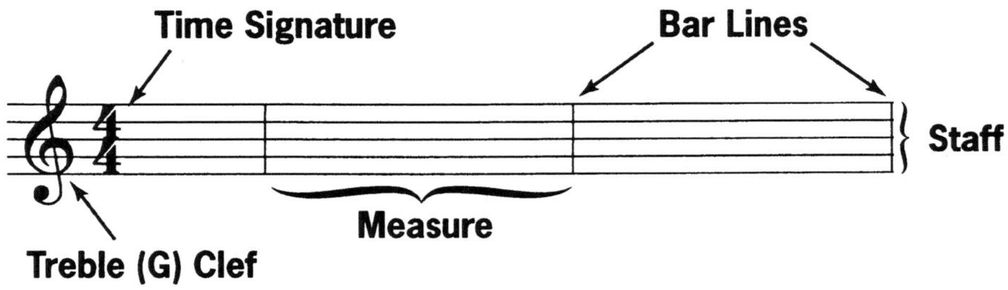

The top number in the time signature indicates the number of beats in each measure. The bottom number in the time signature indicates what type of note gets one beat. If the bottom number is a 4, the quarter note gets one beat. If the bottom number is an 8, the eighth note gets one beat, etc. If "C" is written, the piece is in 4/4. C stands for **common time**.

Strum Bars

A **chord** is when three or more strings are played at the same time. Often, when playing chords, the strings are strummed. For the exercises and songs in this book, the chords will be strummed with a pick. For the holding position of the pick, see page 7. When strumming, the right-hand wrist rotates slightly, and the arm moves from the elbow as the pick moves across the strings. When strumming the strings down, be sure to strum straight down. Do not strum outward. Written below are several strum bar signs. Each is a down strum, but the length of the strum varies. The time value of each strum is written to the side. This mark, ⊓, written above the strum bar, indicates a downstroke. If the strum gets more than one beat, strum the strings on the first beat, and allow them to ring for the additional beats. Practice playing each strum bar several times while strumming all six strings open. **Open** means that no left-hand fingers are pushing on the strings.

 = 1 beat

 = 2 beats

 = 3 beats

 = 4 beats

Practice the following rhythm exercise strumming all six strings open. Strumming the strings open may seem a bit strange at first, but the object is to play the correct rhythm and not be concerned with holding chords. Tap your foot on the beat (four times in each measure). The pick should be used to do the strum.

Open Chords

Shown below are numerous open chords. Open chords are chords that utilize strings that are not pressed down ("open strings") with the left-hand fingers. These chords are commonly used in country and folk tunes and are effective chords to use when accompanying a singer.

Major Chords

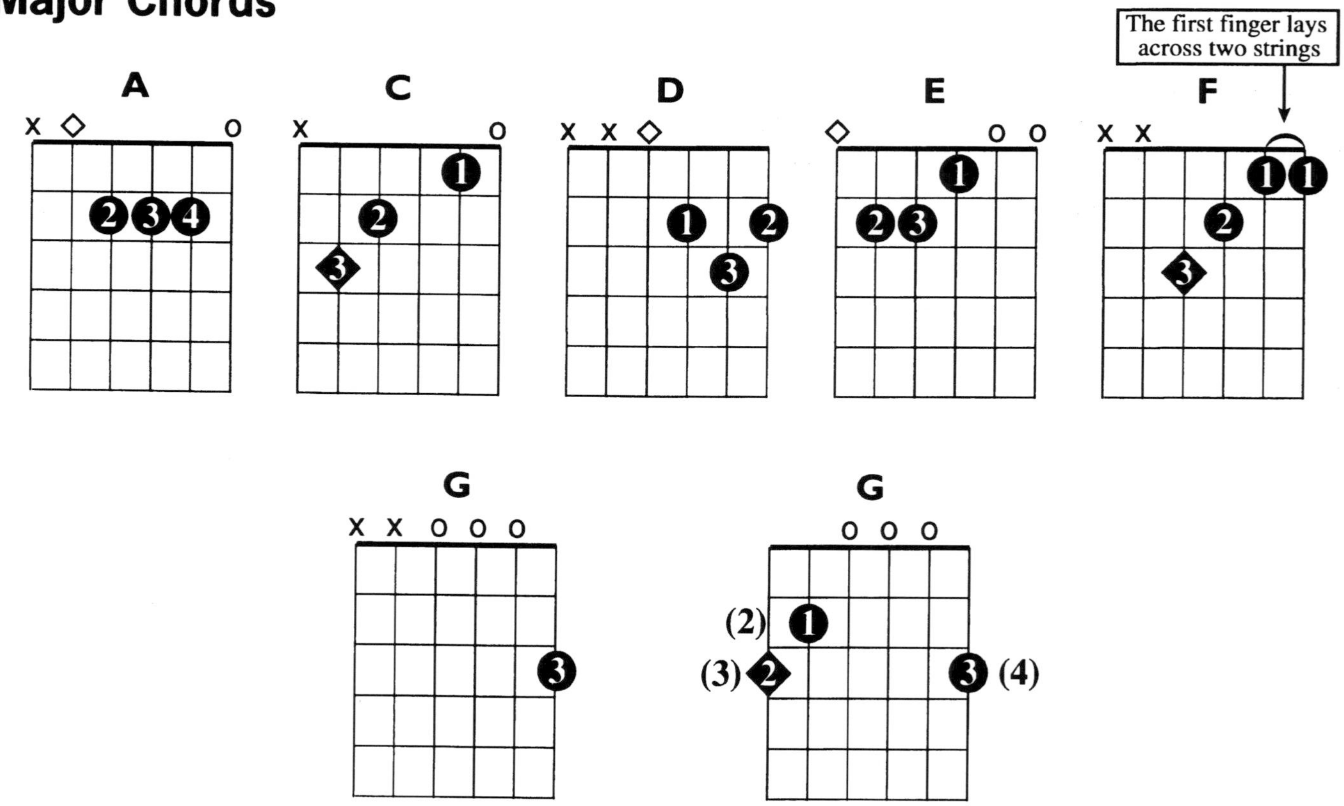

Minor Chords

Am

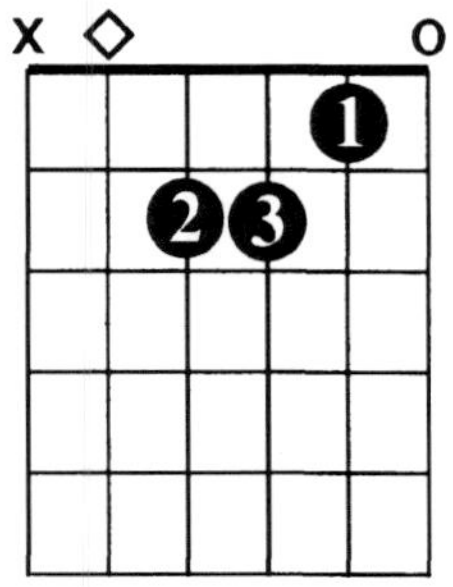

Bm

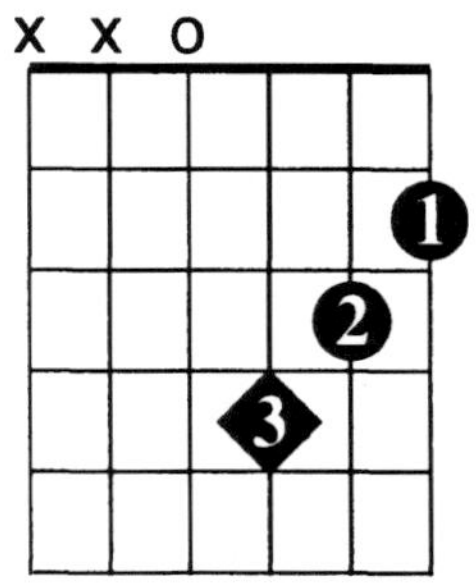

Dm

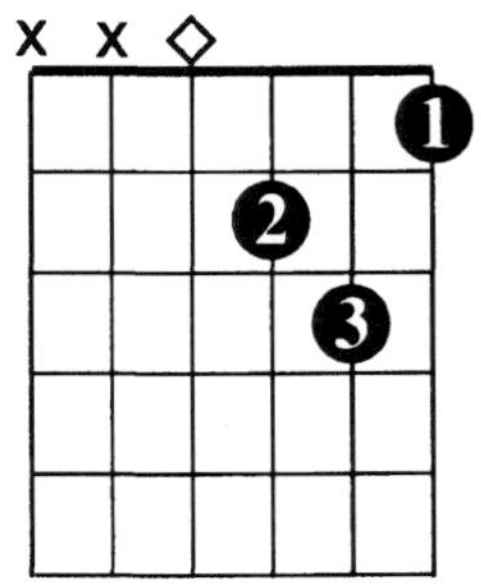

Em

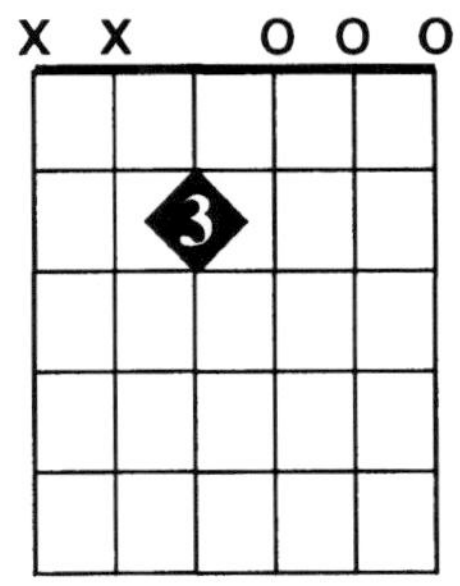

Em

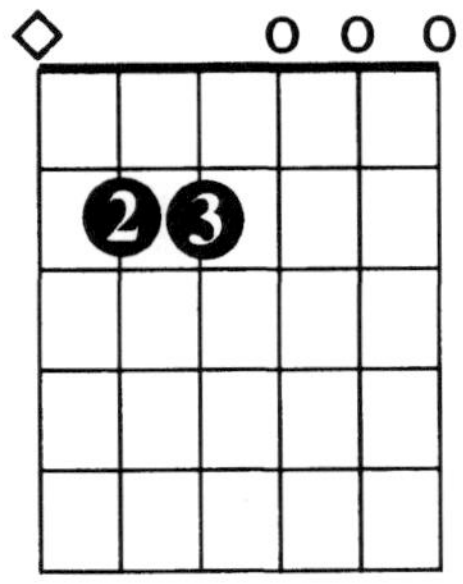

Seventh Chords

A7

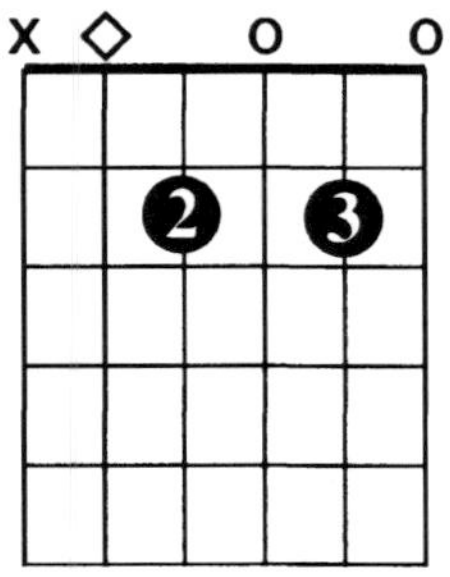

B7

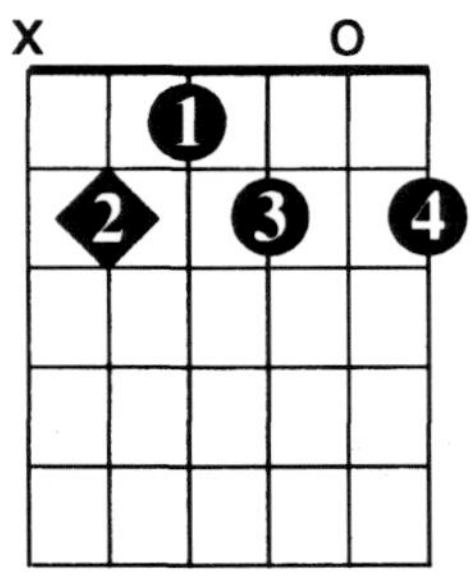

C7

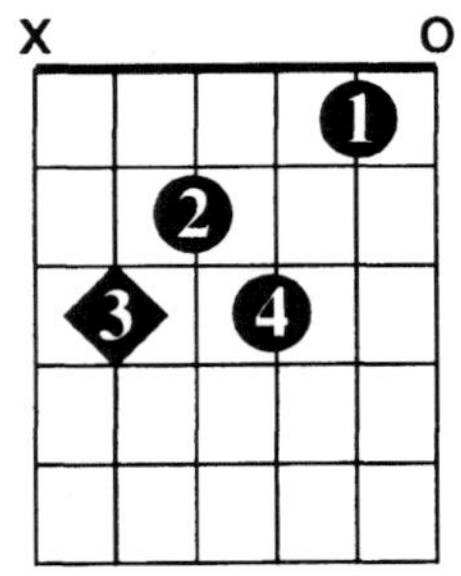

D7

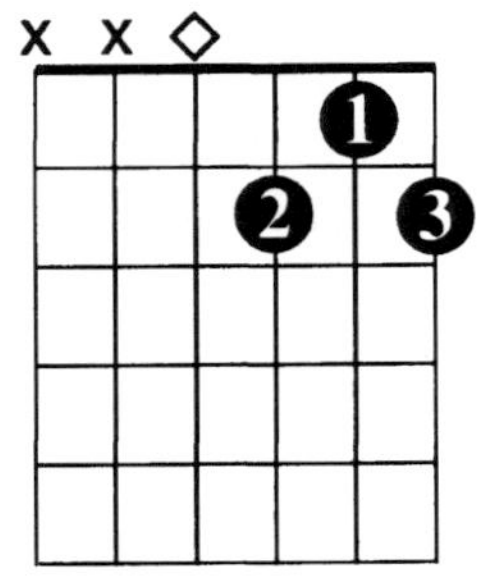

E7

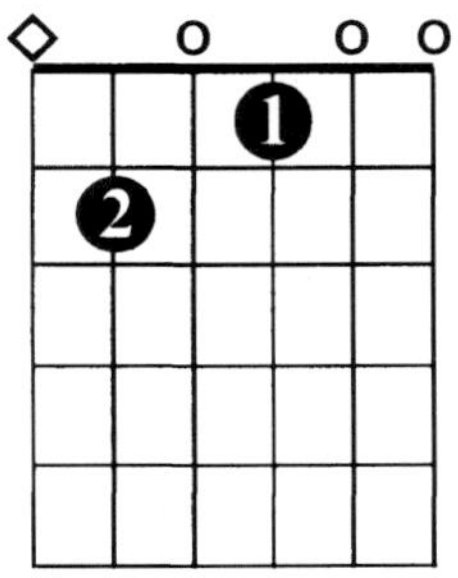

G7

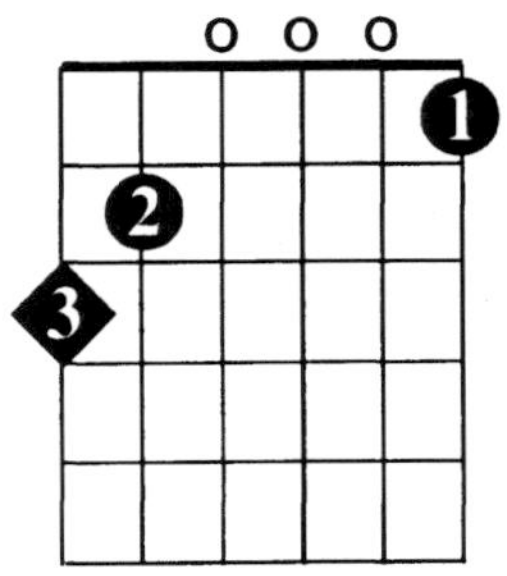

Practice the following exercises using down strums to gain control of the open chords. Each chord is assigned a quarter-note strum bar and should be strummed once for each beat. If strum bars are not present in each measure, play the strum pattern that is presented at the beginning of the progression.

Exercise 1

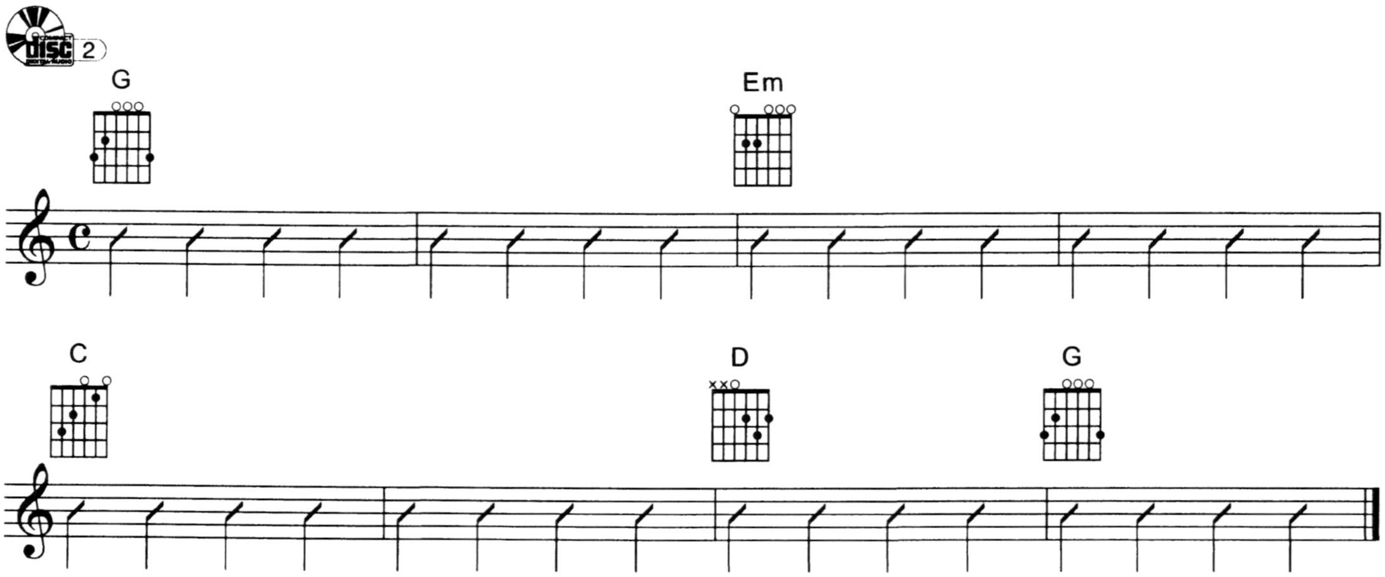

Exercise 2

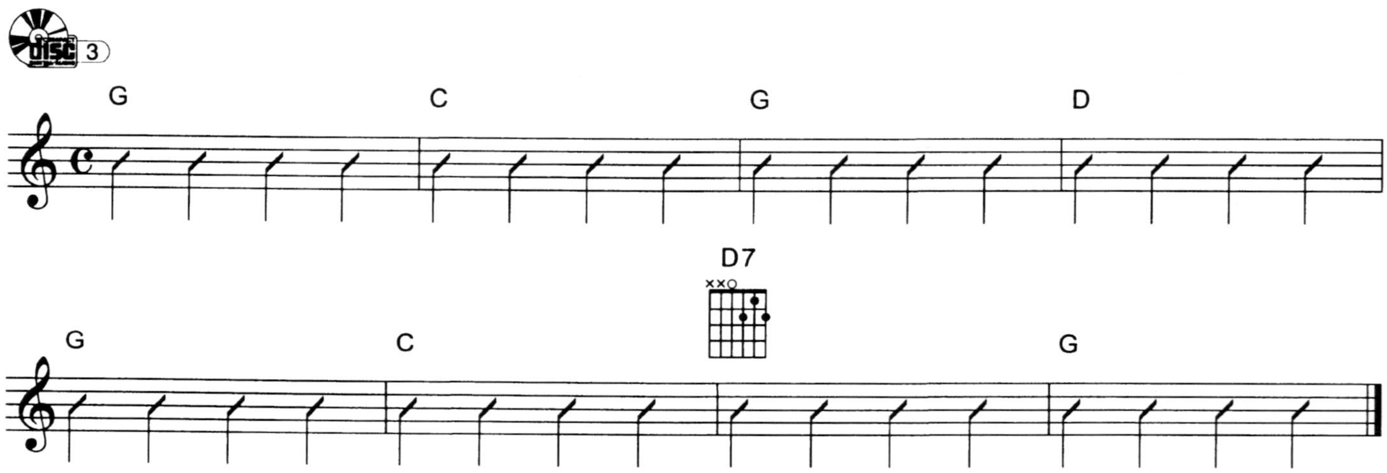

Exercise 3

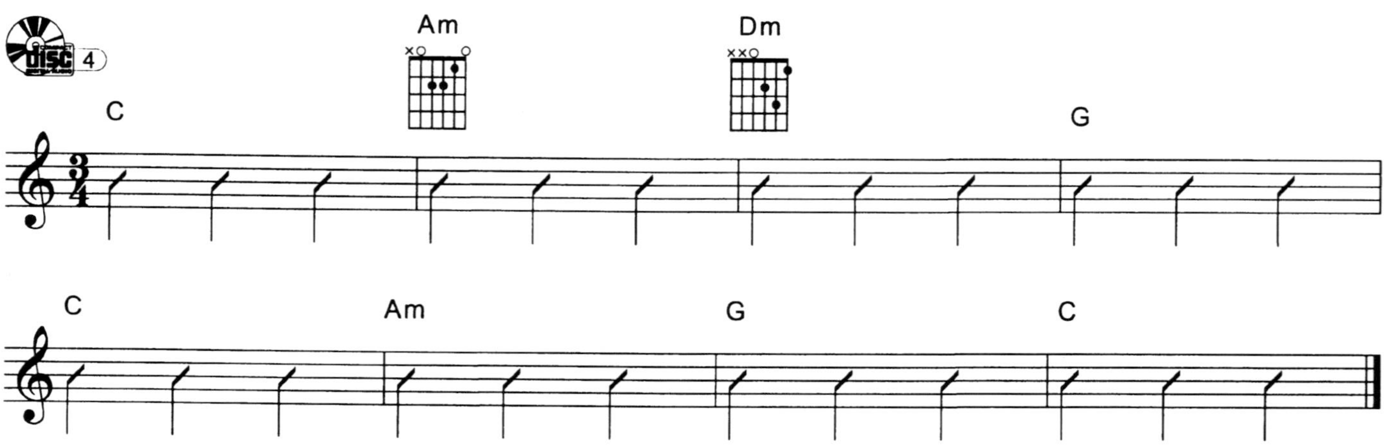

Exercise 4

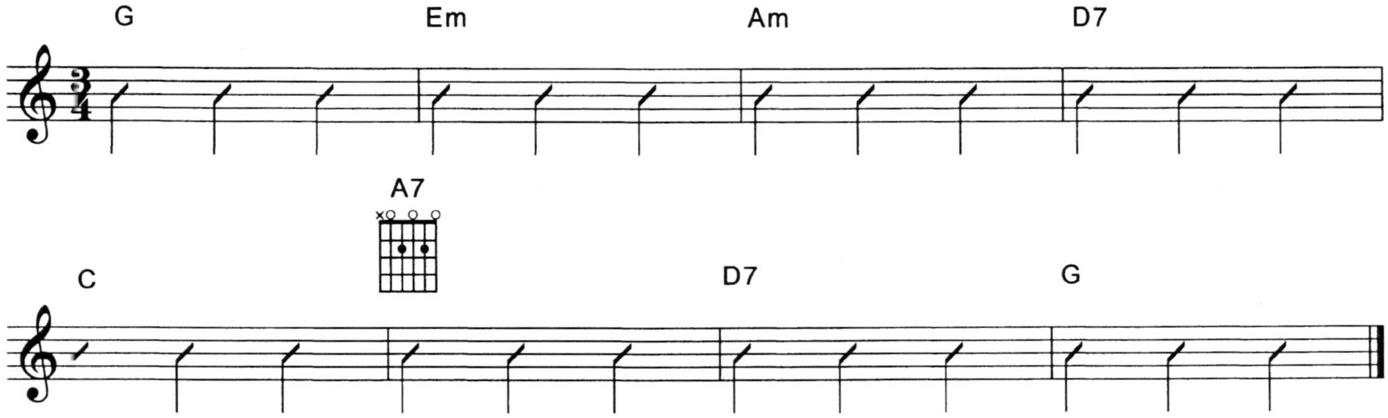

To master chord changes which are difficult, simply pick two chords and strum them two times each moving back and forth from chord to chord. Repeat this exercises by mixing and matching different chord combinations. Students may use this exercise to master any part of their rhythm guitar playing such as new strum patterns and fingerpicking patterns. Students may wish to create practice progressions of their own to master these chords. Changing chords smoothly will be a result of practicing correctly. Be sure to practice at a slow tempo to ensure smooth and clear chord changes.

This :‖ is a repeat sign. When it appears, go to the double bar with the dots on the right ‖: and play that portion of the piece again. If there is not a set of double bars with dots on the right, repeat the beginning of the piece.

Exercise 5

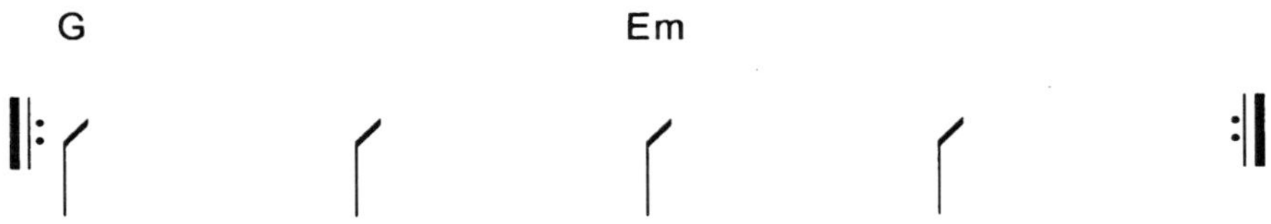

Exercise 6

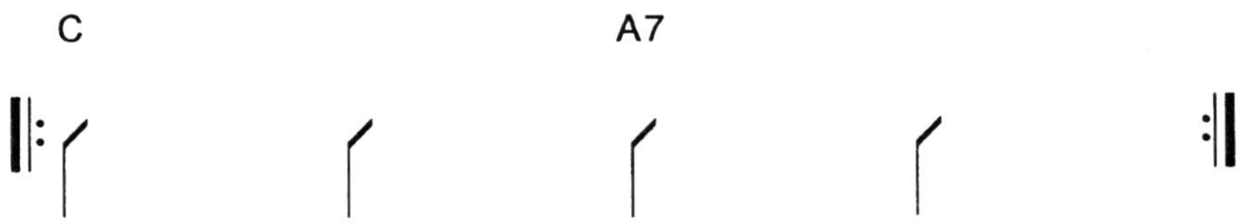

Exercise 7

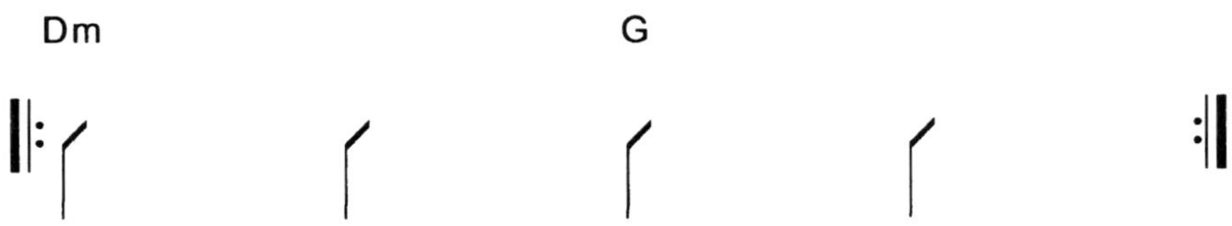

Using open chords, play the following tunes.

Aura Lee

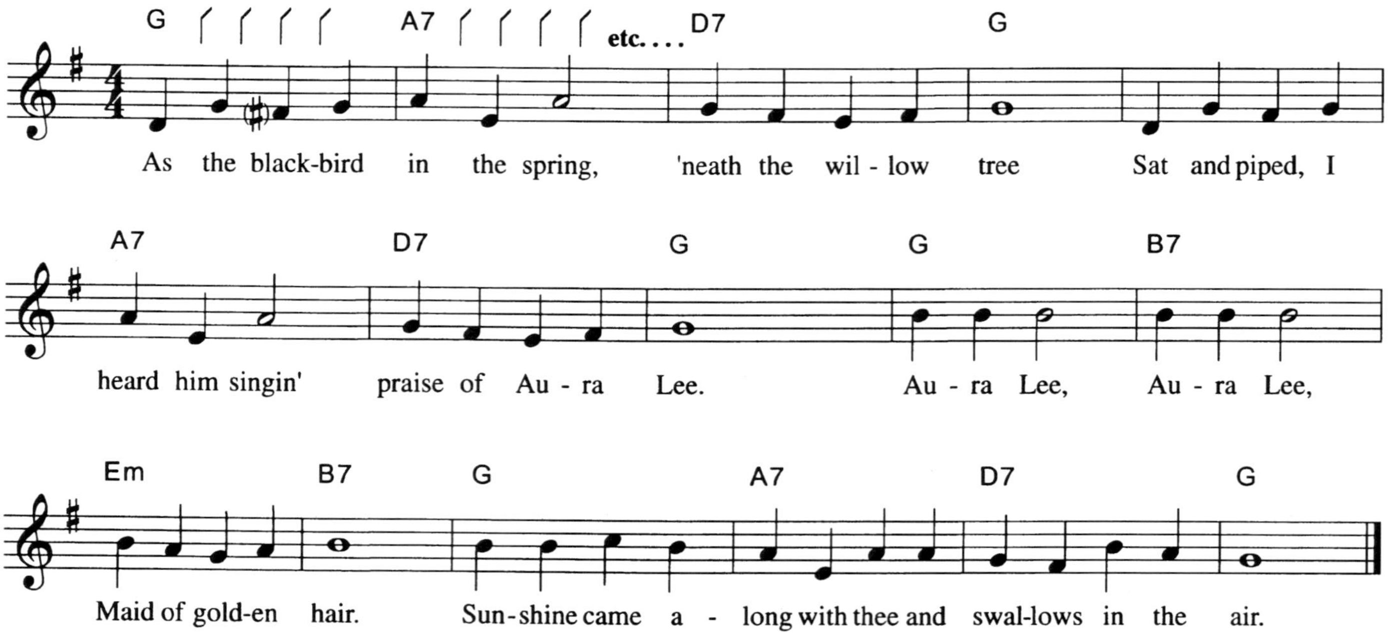

Amazing Grace

If a song begins with an incomplete measure, these notes are called ***pick-up*** notes. The missing beats are in the last measure.

When two different chords are in the same measure simply divide the measure in half and assign the appropriate number of strums (beats) to each chord. In the case of 3/4 time, determine which chord gets the majority of the beats by where it is located above the measure and give it two beats. The other chord will receive one beat.

Exercise 8

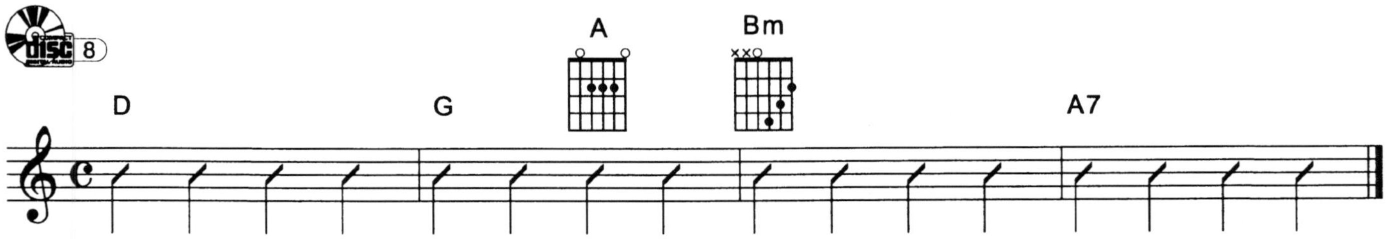

Exercise 9

Exercise 10

By learning new strum patterns, more variety and excitement can be added to one's rhythm guitar playing. Many strum patterns are shown below. As a rule of thumb, the second of two eighth notes that are joined by a flag will be strummed up (⊓ V / 1 &). Only the first few strings (strings 1-3 and maybe 4) need to be plucked when strumming up. The following strum patterns will help guitarists create exciting accompaniment parts and break the monotony of down strums.

Before learning the new strum patterns, play the following chord progressions using only down-up strumming.

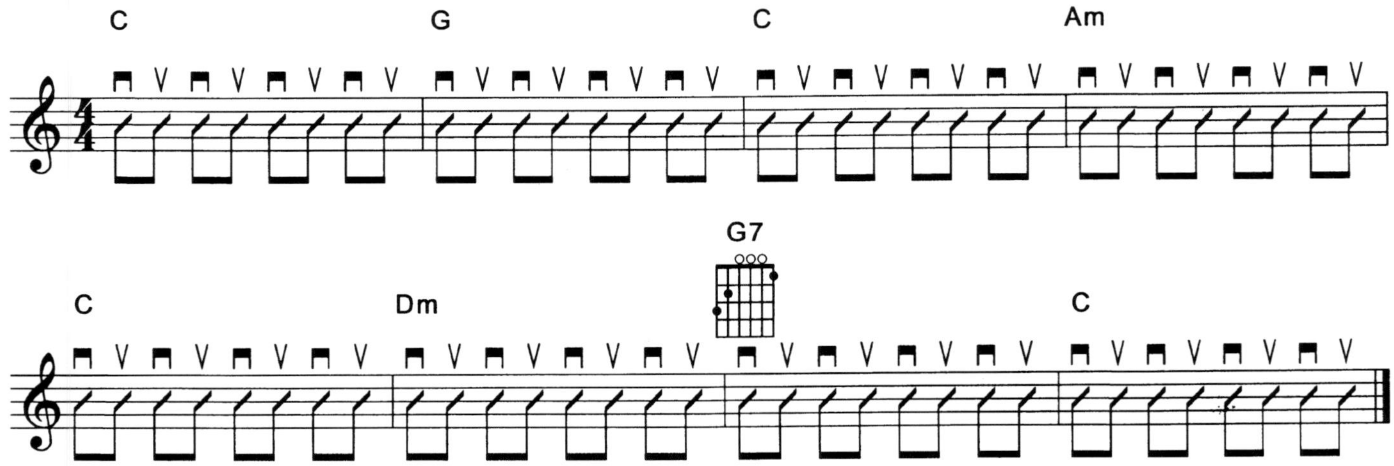

Written below are eight strum patterns. Each of the strum patterns take one measure of 4/4 or 3/4 to complete and can be used with any folk tune. Once a pattern has been selected, play the same pattern in each measure of the piece.

Practice holding any chord and play each pattern. Be careful to use the correct strum direction and correct rhythm. Tap your foot on each beat and count the rhythms aloud. The patterns are written in order of difficulty. Master one pattern before moving to the next.

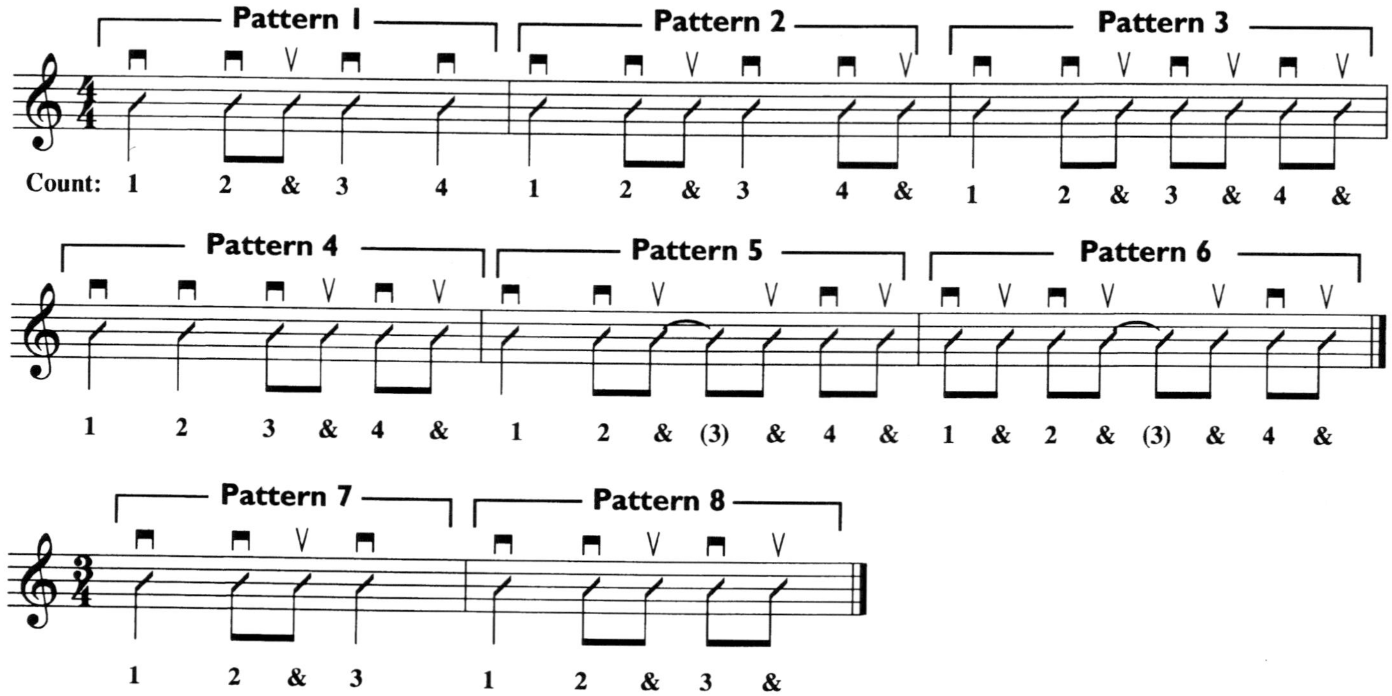

Notice pattern six contains a loop called a "tie." When two strum bars or two of the same notes are connected with a tie, play the first strum and allow it to ring through the time value of the second. Do not strum the second strum bar.

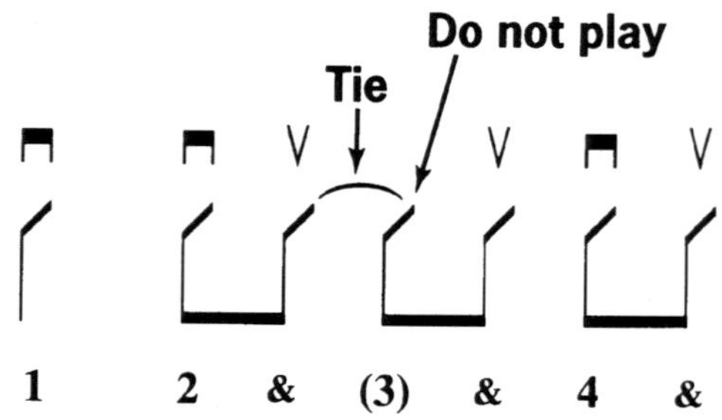

When two chords appear in a measure with more active strum patterns, simply repeat the process for two chords in a measure for down strums only. If a strum patterns has a tie between beats two and three, it is common to anticipate the second chord in the measure by playing it on the "and" of two.

Use the following chord progressions to practice new strum patterns. Students may also use the chord progressions presented earlier in the book to practice the new strum patterns.

She'll Be Comin' Round the Mountain

Streets of Laredo

He's Got the Whole World

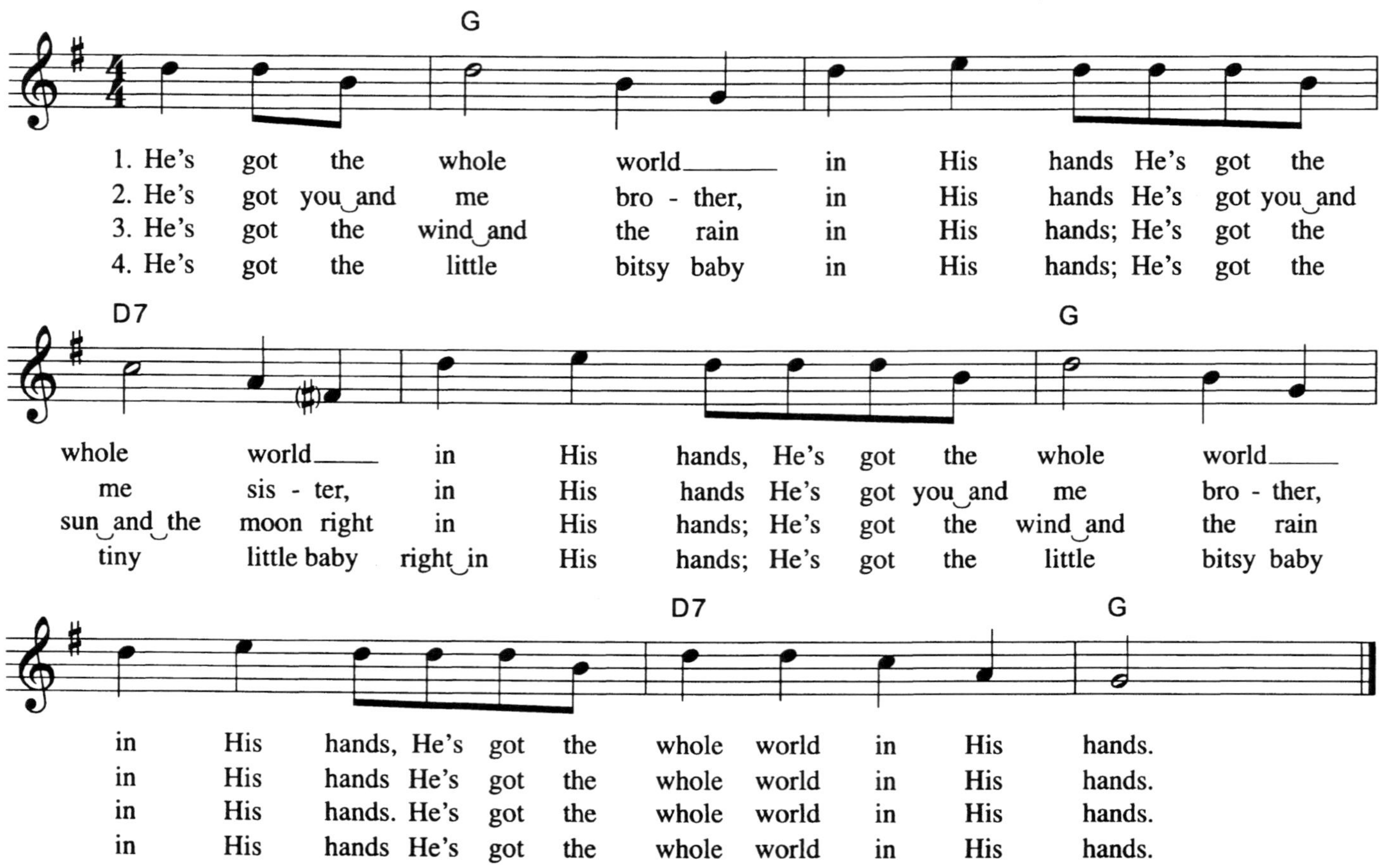

Midnight Special Blues

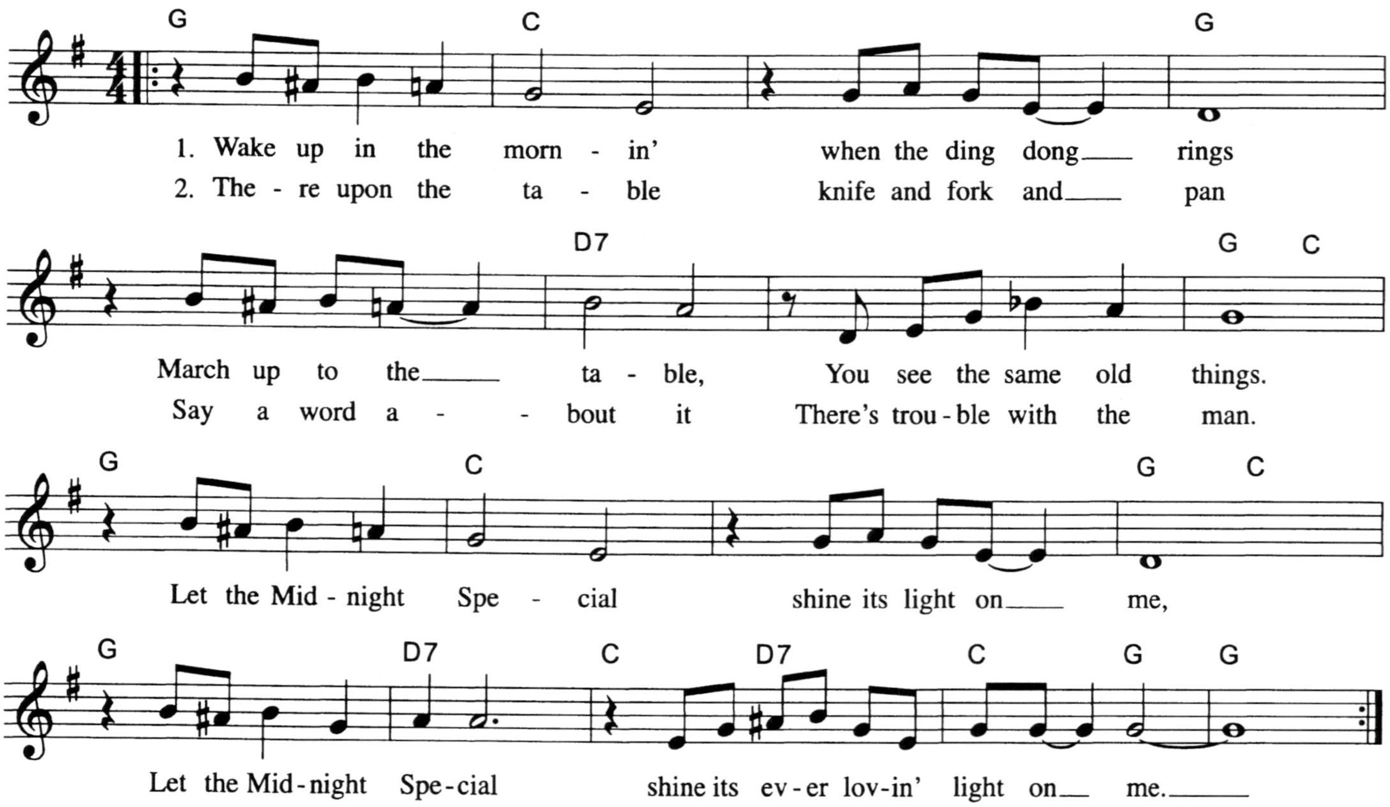

How to Read Standard Notation

Being able to read and write music in standard notation will be a great asset to any guitarist. Understanding standard notation makes it easier for guitarists to learn new music (especially if a recording is not available), write their ideas for other guitarists to play, and jot down ideas they may want to remember in the future.

The lines and spaces on which notes are written is called the **staff**. Guitar music is written in the **treble clef**. The treble clef sign will be at the beginning of the staff for music played on the guitar. The treble clef circles and identifies the second line from the botton as G. The treble clef is sometimes called the **G clef**.

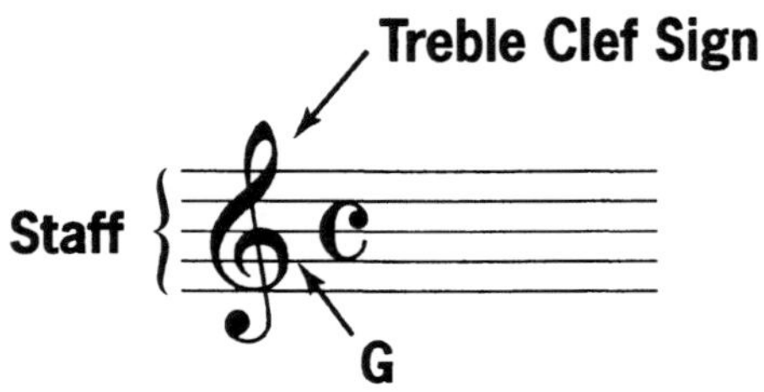

The note names for the treble clef are shown on the staff below. The mnemonic (memory building) device commonly used to remember the notes on the lines of the treble clef is ***E**very **G**ood **B**oy **D**oes **F**ine*. The letters found in the spaces of the treble clef spell the word ***FACE***.

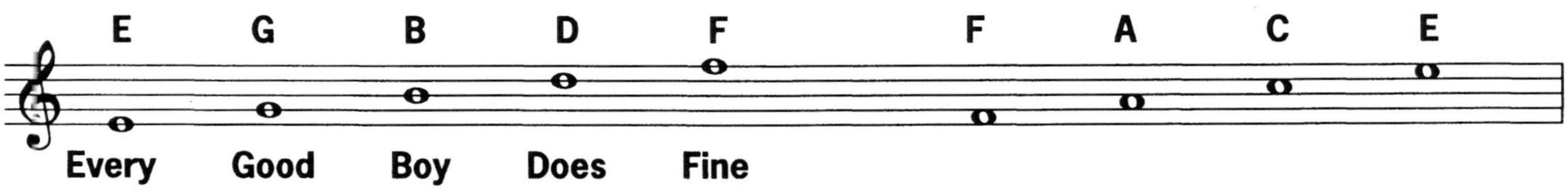

The time values are the same for standard notation as they are for strumming notation. Time values for each note and rest are shown below for time signatures with a four as the bottom number (4/4, 3/4, 2/4 etc.)

= **Whole Note — 4 beats**

= **Half Note — 2 beats**

= **Dotted Half Note — 3 beats (The dot adds to a note 1/2 its original value)**

= **Quarter Note — 1 beat**

= **Dotted Quarter Note — 1 1/2 beats**

= **Eighth Note — 1/2 beat**

= **Sixteenth Note — 1/4 beat**

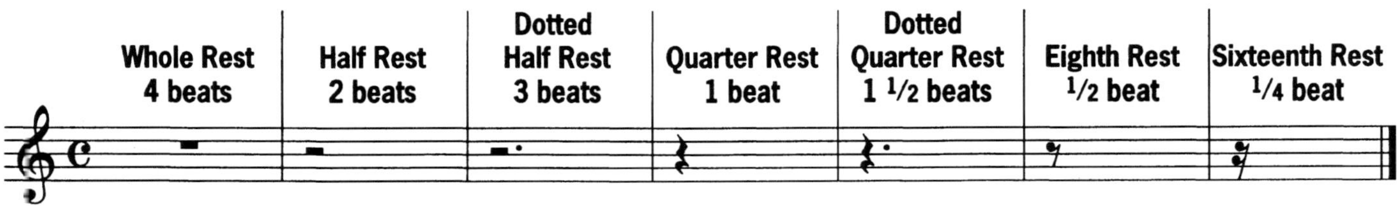

Standard Notation in First Position

While there are many notes on the guitar (one note for each string and fret), only standard notation in first position will be covered in this book. The term **first position** means that the first finger of the left hand will be stationed or positioned at the first fret and will, therefore, play all the notes on each string located in that fret. This allows each of the left-hand fingers to play in the fret that corresponds with the finger number. The second finger is responsible for all of the notes in the second fret; the third finger plays the notes in the third fret and the fourth finger will play the notes found in the fourth fret. When playing in a higher position, the first finger determines the position, and the other fingers correspond to the frets just as they did in first position. For example, to play in the fifth position, the first finger of the left hand is stationed at the fifth fret, the second finger in the sixth fret, the third finger in the seventh fret and the fourth finger in the eighth fret. Sometimes a Roman numeral is used in music and chord diagrams to indicate a position or fret number.

Notes on the First String

The notes on the first string are shown below. They are E, F, and G. This following exercise will help in the memorization of these notes.

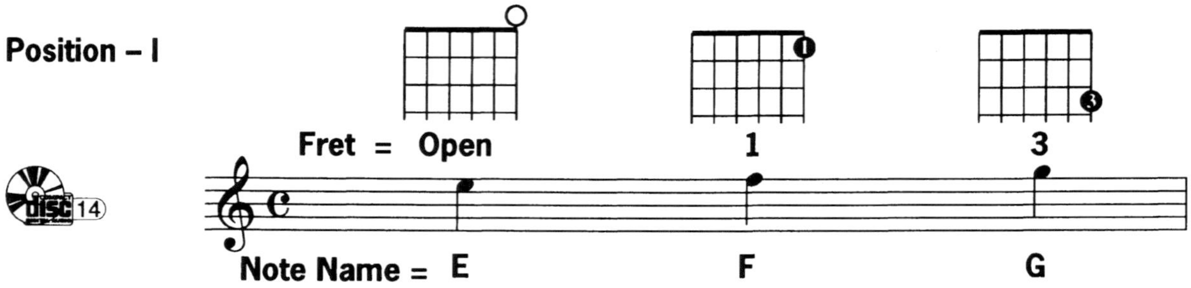

Notes on the Second String

The notes on the second string are shown below. They are B, C, and D. This following exercise will help in the memorization of these notes.

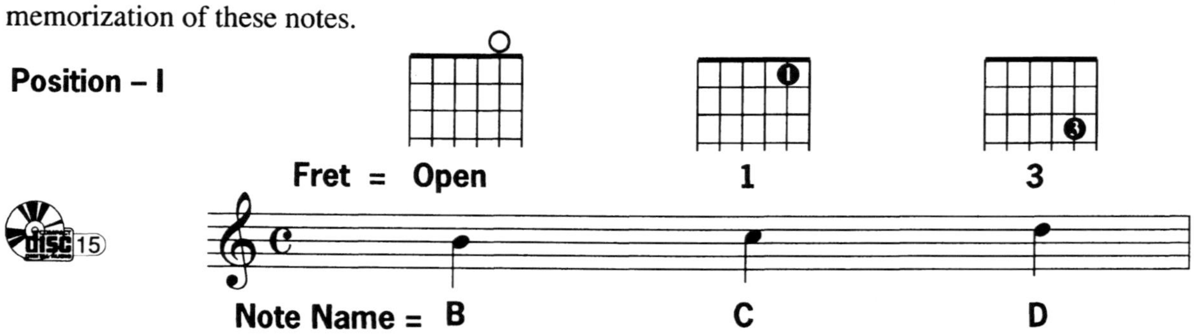

This is a tie. When it connects two notes of the same pitch, the first note rings through the value of the second note. The second note is not played. Also see page 18.

When playing a series of eighth notes, alternate picking (down-up picking) is used. The first of two eighth notes is picked with a downstroke (⊓). The second note is picked up with an upstroke (V). *Folks Wagon* makes use of eighth notes.

Folks Wagon

16

Eighth Rest. Rest for 1/2 Beat.
The note following this rest sign is played on the second half of the beat and is played with an upstroke

Notes on the Third String

The notes G and A are found on the third string.

Position – I

17

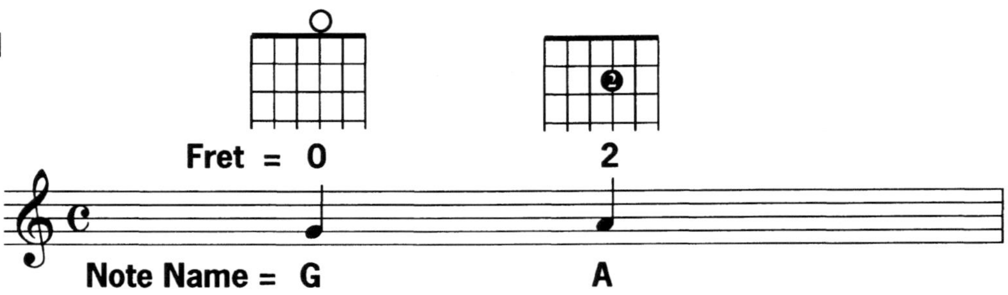

Play the following melody that uses the notes found on the first three strings.

Red River Valley

18

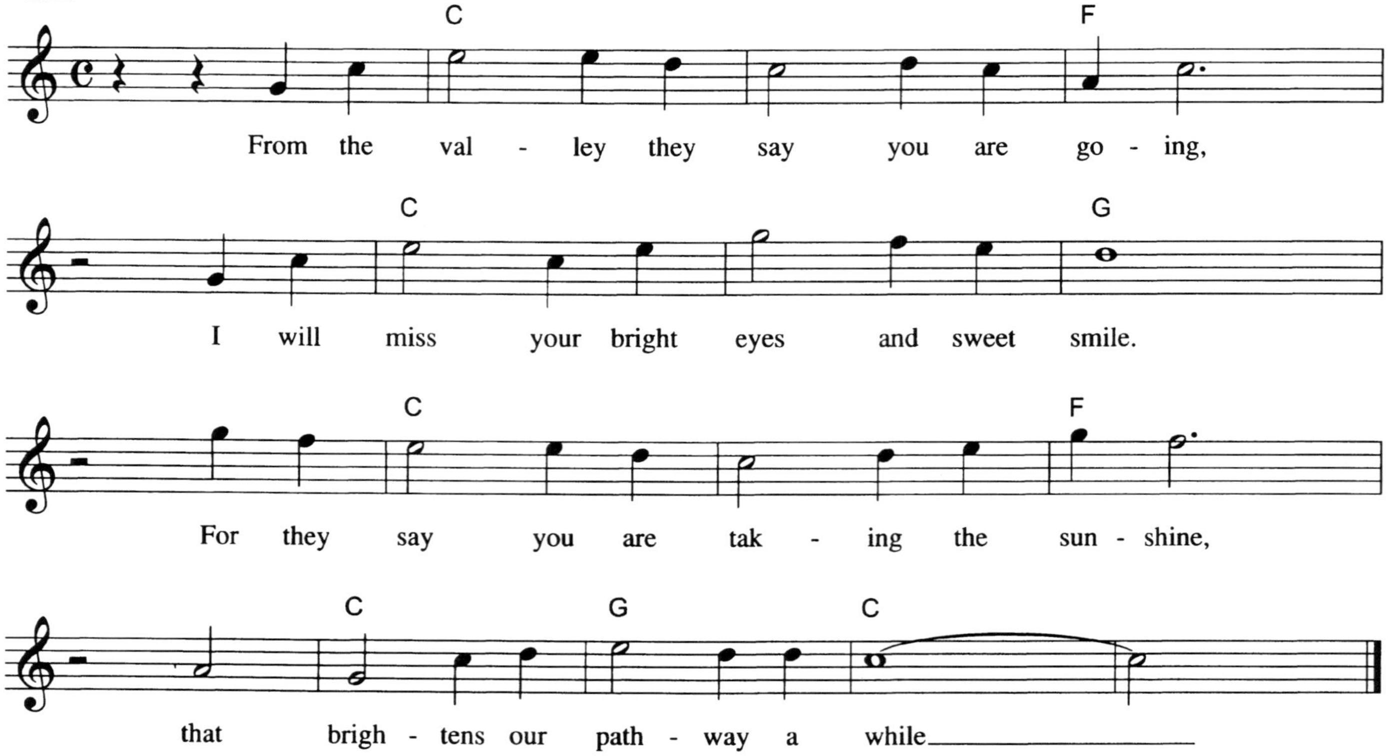

Notes on the Fourth String

The notes on the fourth string are D, E, and F.

Position – I

19

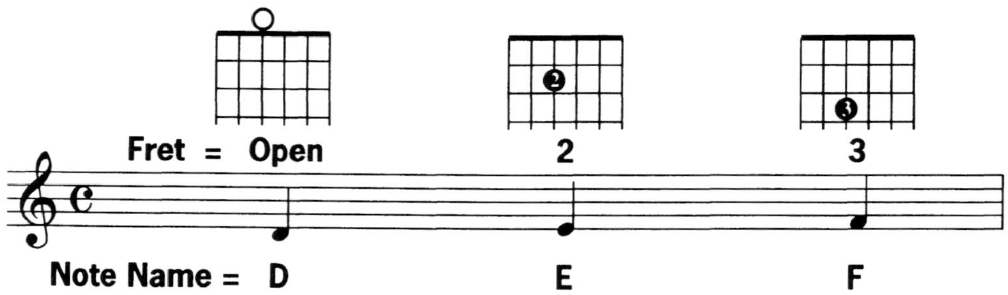

An accidental is a sign that alters the pitch of a note. The sharp sign (♯), flat sign (♭) and natural sign (♮) are all accidentals. When a sharp sign appears in front of a note, the note is raised one fret (one half step). If an F on the first string has a sharp sign in front of it, move one fret higher (toward the body of the guitar). The note, F-sharp, will be played on the first string, second fret. If an open note (a note that is usually played on an open string) is sharped, play the note in the first fret of the same string. When playing notes with accidentals, be sure the finger number matches the fret number.

When a note has an accidental, the accidental affects **all** of the notes with the same pitch in the remainder of that measure only. After that measure, the accidental is negated and the notes return to their original pitch. A natural sign in front of a note cancels the sharp or flat.

Fret 0 4 0 4 0 4 3 2 0 4 4 0

When a flat sign appears in front of a note, the note is lowered one fret (one half step). For example, if a D on the second string has a flat sign in front of it, play it one fret lower (toward the head of the guitar). The note D-flat will be played on the second string, second fret. If an open note has a flat in front of it, the note must be moved to a lower string as an open string cannot be lowered without retuning. To flat an open note, place a finger on the next lower string in the fret that matches the pitch of the note on the open string. Then flat the note by lowering it one fret. A chart showing the location of all the flatted open notes is shown below.

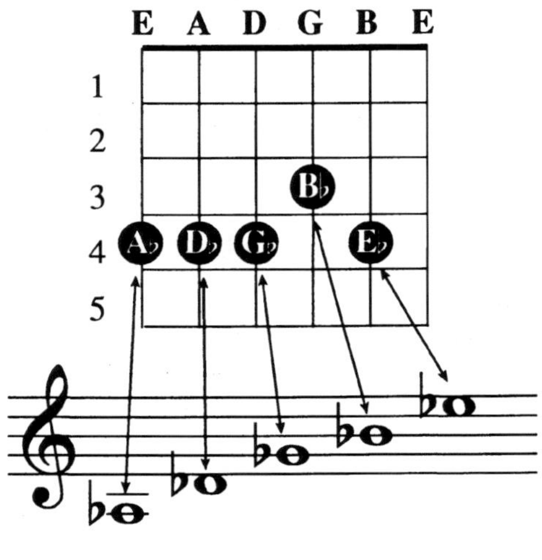

Fret: 3 2 1 3 0 3 0 0 4 4 4 0 0 3 0 3 3

Note: If accidentals appear after the clef sign, [key signature with sharps] or [key signature with flats], this is called a **Key Signature**. The note names of the lines and spaces where the accidentals are placed should be altered throughout the piece in all octaves.

Notes on the Fifth String

The notes on the fifth string are written below. Remember, use the same left-hand finger number as the fret number.

Position – I

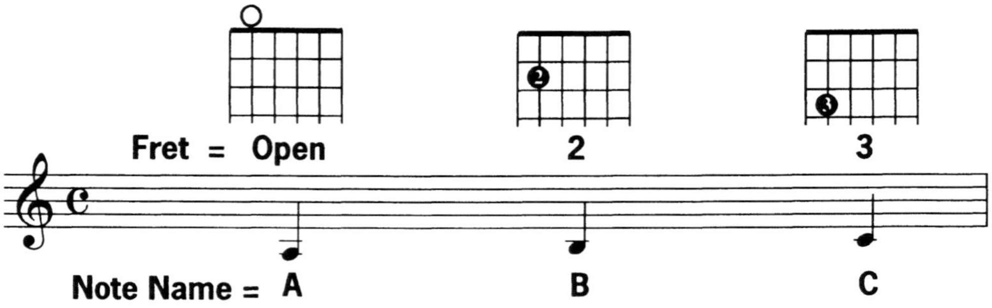

Practice the following exercise which uses only the notes on the fifth string.

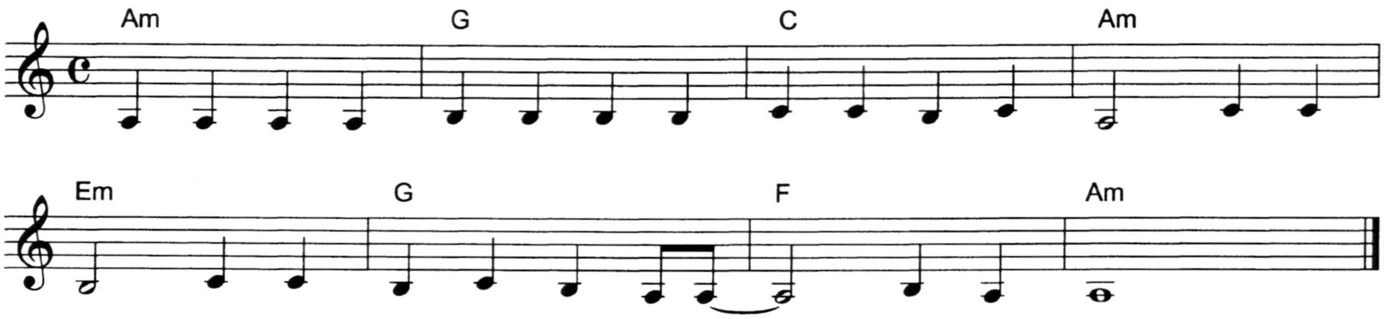

Notes on the Sixth String

Written below are the notes on the sixth string.

Position – I

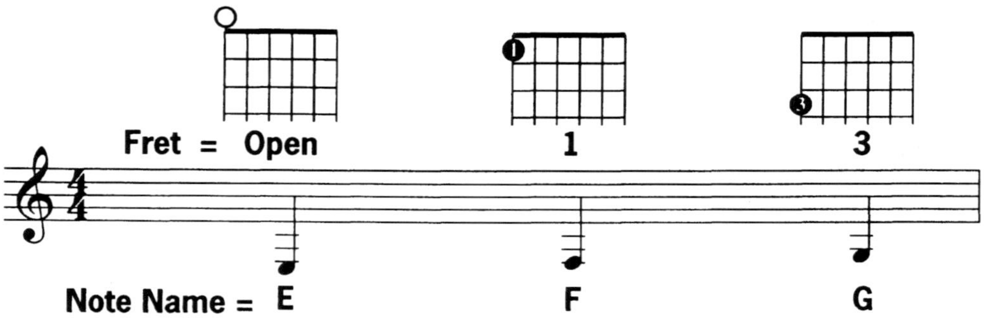

Practice the following exercise using only the notes on the sixth string.

Practice the following solo which uses the notes on strings four, five and sixth.

Oh Susana

22

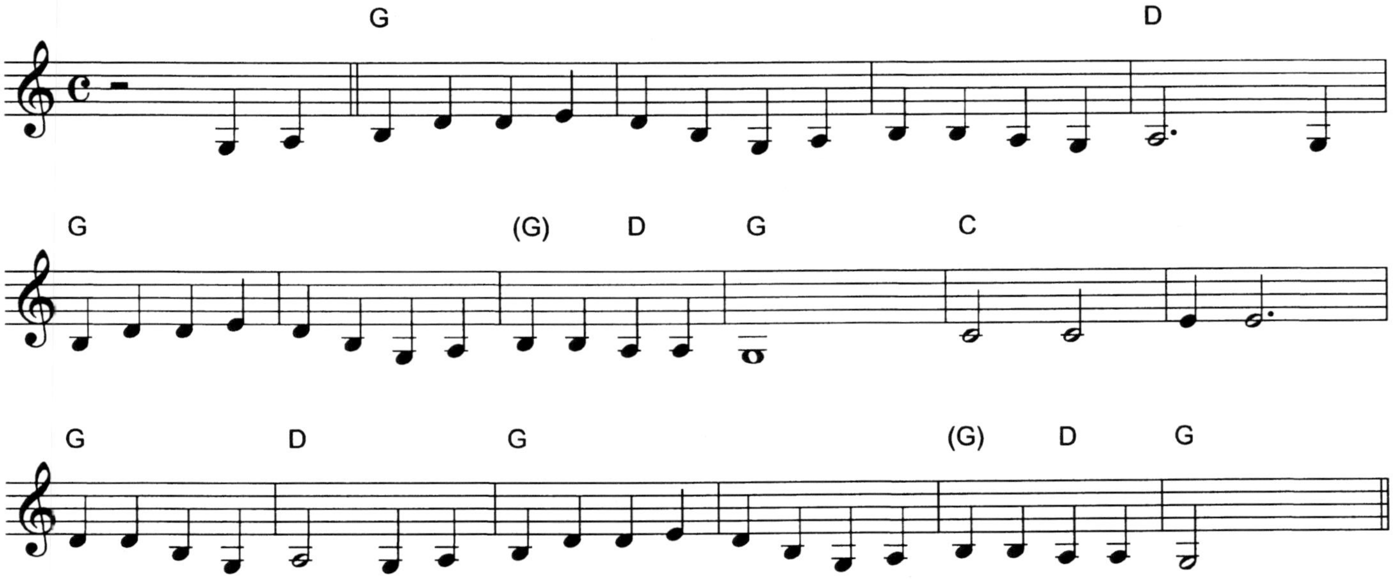

Tablature

Another way of writing guitar music is called tablature. The six horizontal lines represent the strings on a guitar. The top line is the first string.

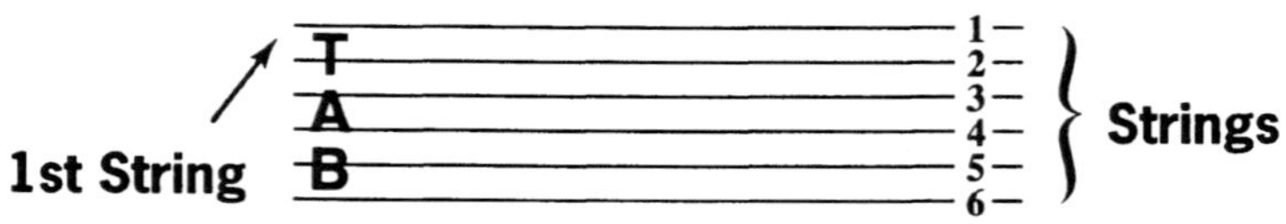

A number on a line indicates in which fret to place a left-hand finger. A stem connected to the number shows the note gets one beat.

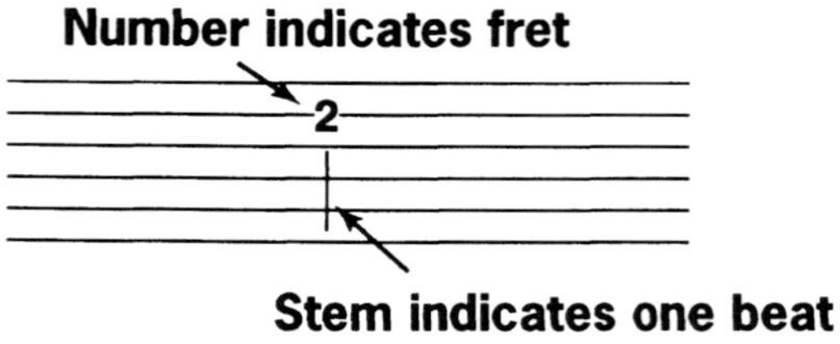

In the example below, the finger would be placed on the first string in the third fret.

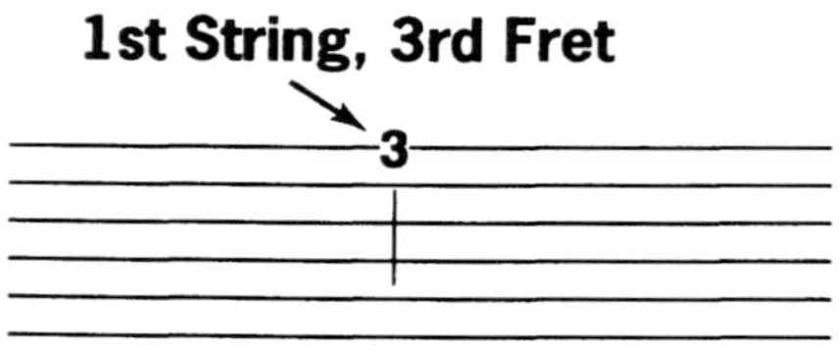

If two or more numbers are written on top of one another, play the strings at the same time.

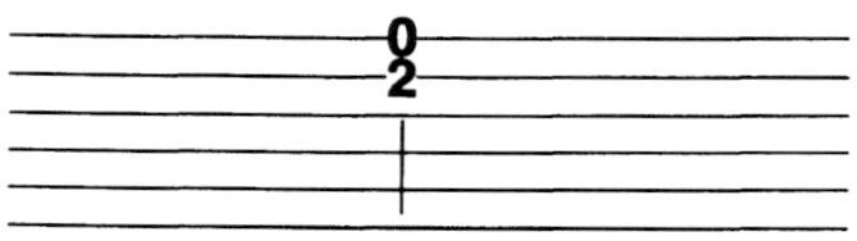

Note Values in Tablature

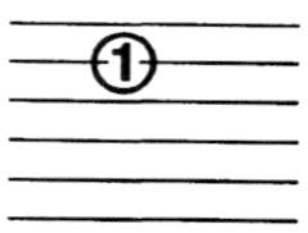

= **Whole Note**

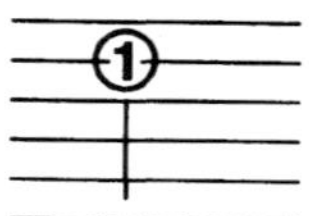

= **Half Note**

= **Quarter Note**

= **Eighth Note**

When the Saints Go Marching In

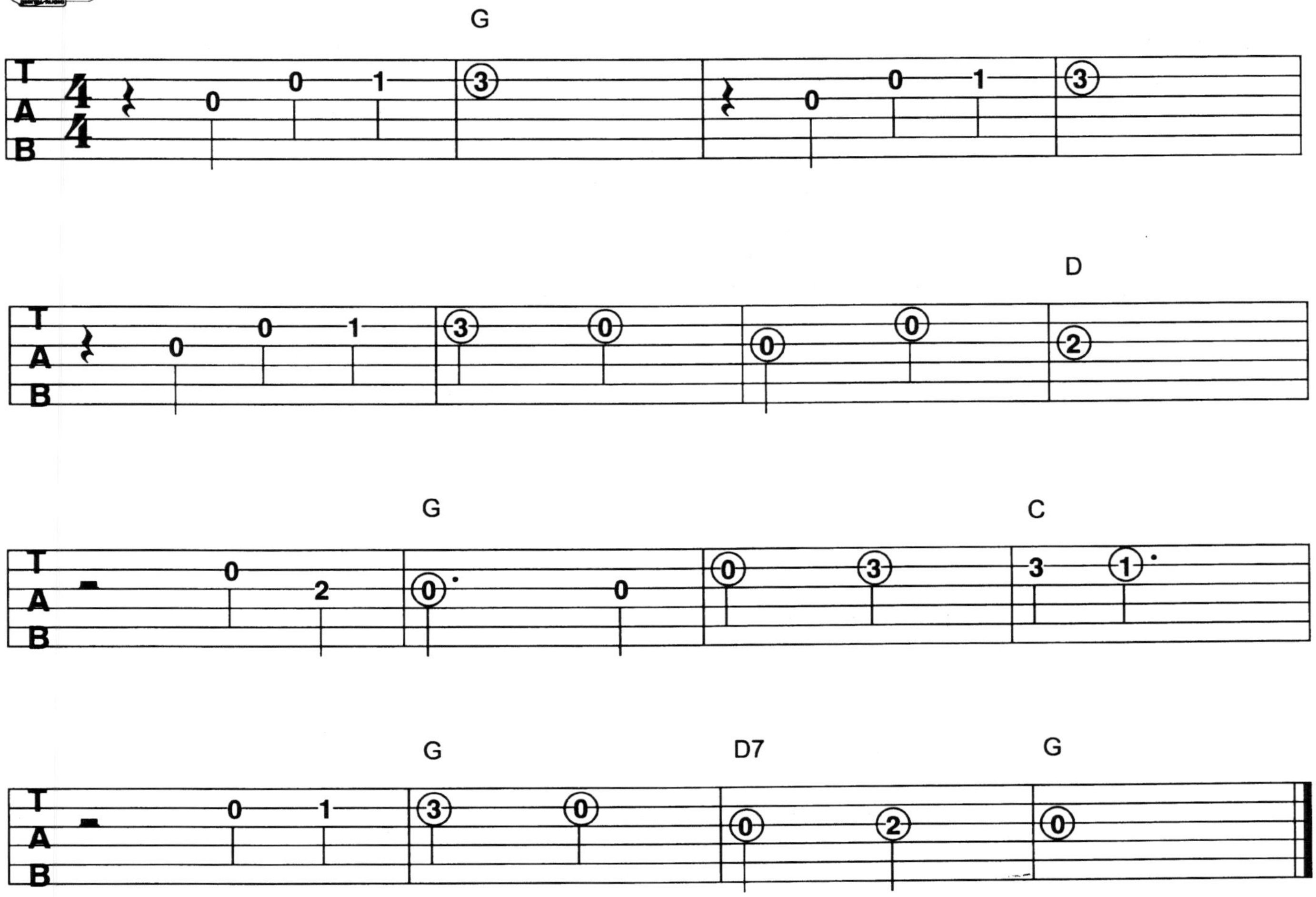

Alternating Bass

Alternating bass is a common accompaniment pattern in folk and country music. As the name implies, the alternating bass strum pattern makes use of a chord's lowest note as well as the chord in it entirety. All of the chords presented in this book can be placed in one of three chord groups based on how many strings are strummed when playing the chord. Those that make use of six strings (G, Em, E7 etc.), those that make use of five strings (Am, A7, C, etc.) and those that make use of four strings (F, Dm, D, etc.). A simple 4/4 alternating bass strum pattern for each chord type is shown below. The number indicates which string is to be plucked by itself while holding the appropriate chord. The strum bar indicates that the chord is to be strummed as it did in the previous chapter on strum patterns.

Pattern for 6-String Chords (G, Em, G7, E, E7)

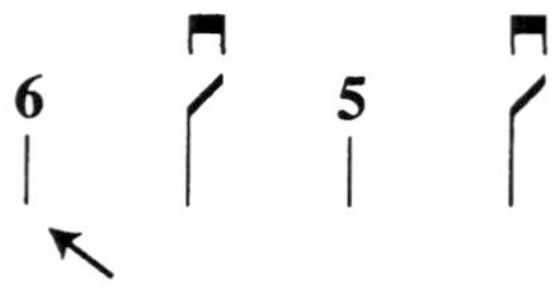

A stem under a number indicates that picking the single string takes one beat. The single string is picked using a down stroke.

Pattern for 5-String Chords (C, A, Am, A7)

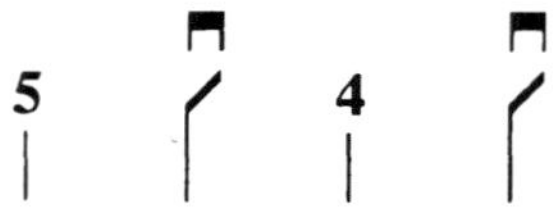

Pattern for 4-String Chords (D, D7, Dm, Bm)

Hold an F chord and try the same pattern. For the 4-string F chord, after playing the 4, move the left hand 3rd finger to the 5th string, 3rd fret to play the 5 (only strum the top three strings.)

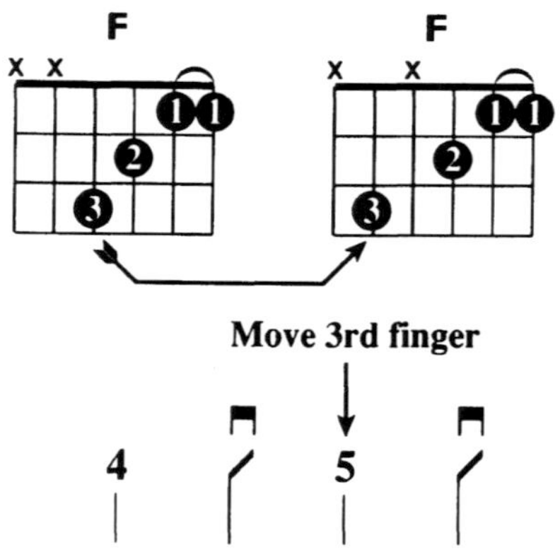

This is a very fun strum pattern to play and it gives the impression that a bass player is playing at the same time. Be sure to use the right pattern (in terms of number of strings) with the right chord. Play the following progressions using this alternating bass pattern. Make sure to play each chord clearly and with a steady beat.

disc 24

①

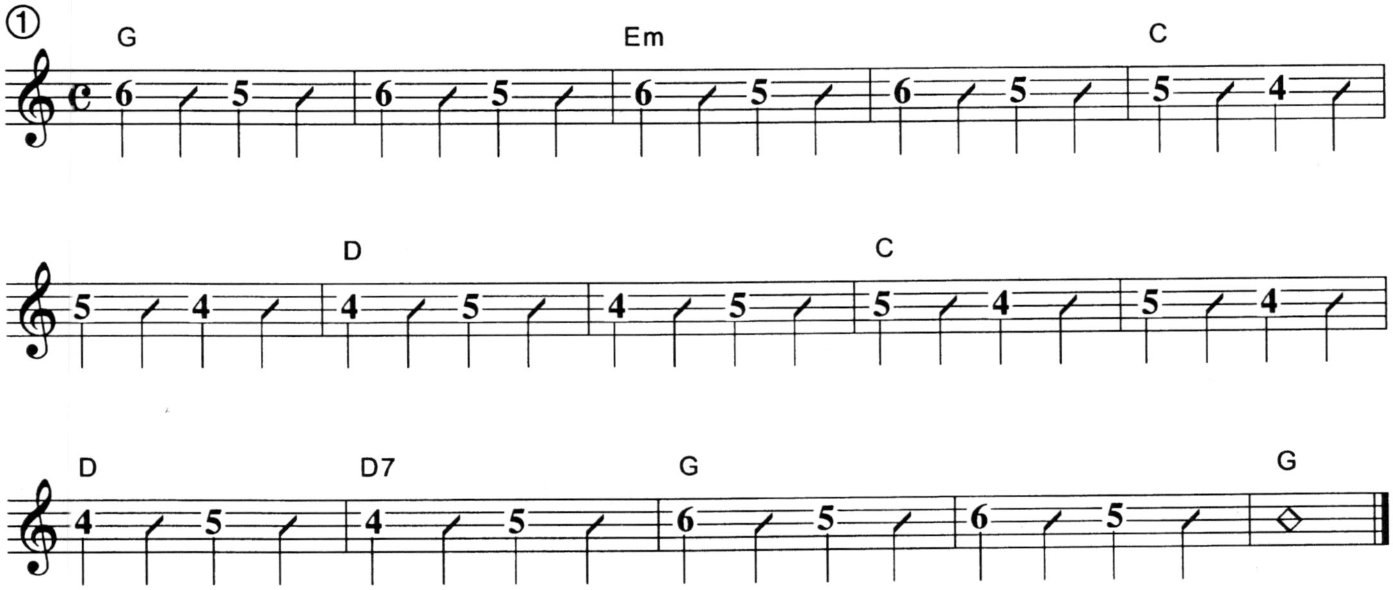

disc 25

②

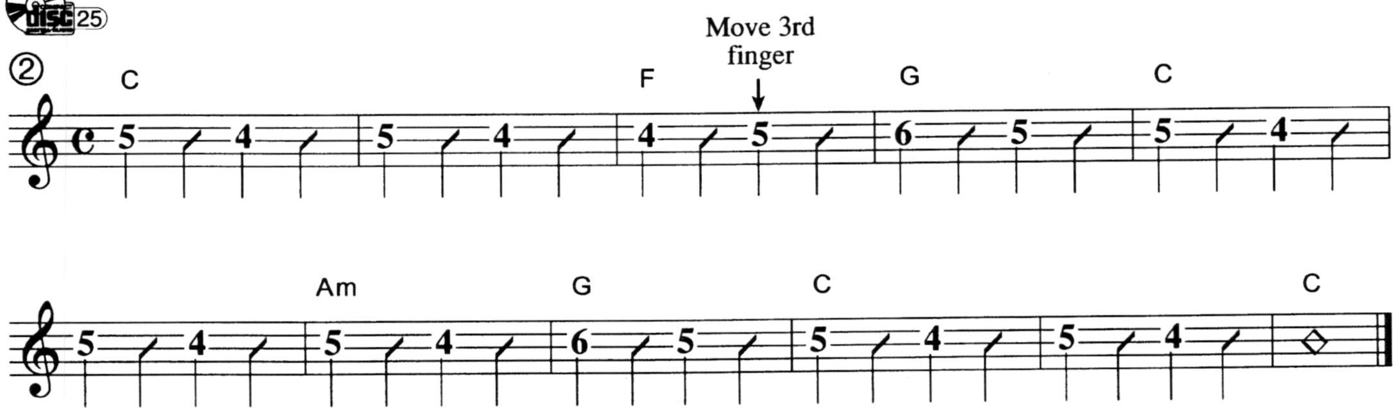

If two chords appear in a measure, play the first half of the pattern for the first chord and then play the first half of the pattern for the second chord in the measure. If C and G appear in the same measure, they will be played as written below.

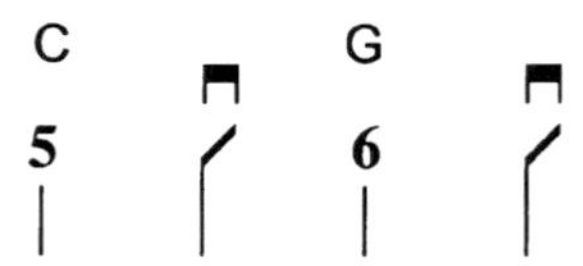

Kum Ba Yah

Here are some variations of the original alternating bass strum pattern.

6-String Patterns

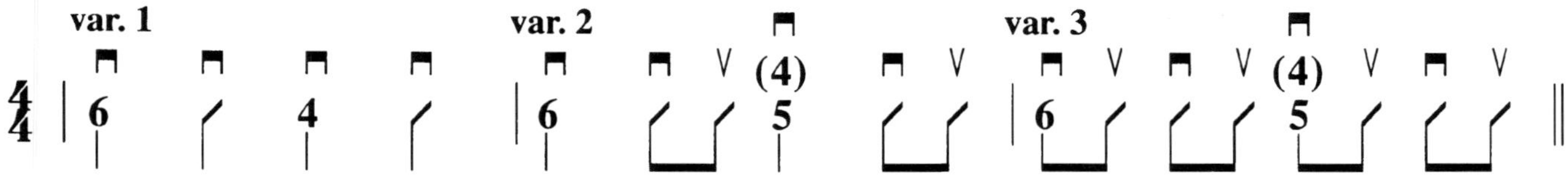

5-String Patterns

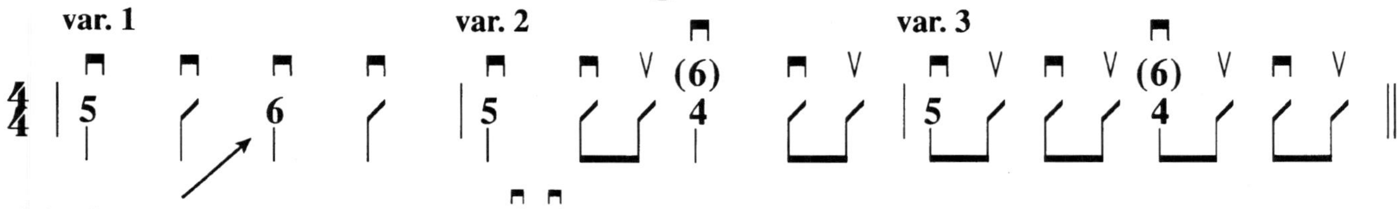

If the C chord is being played after the 5 /, move the 3rd finger of the left hand to the 6th string, 3rd fret to play the 6 /. Strum the top four strings. Then, move it back to play the 5 /.

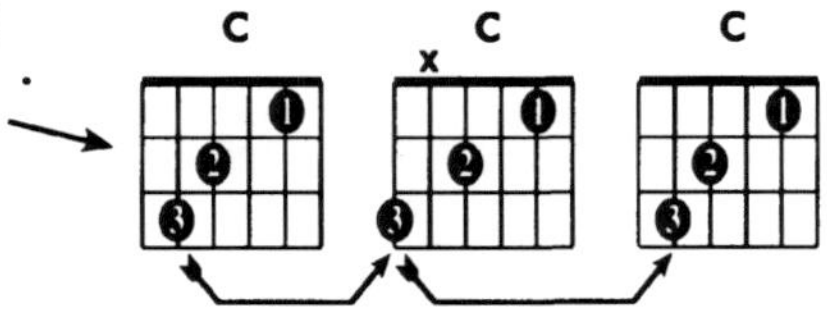

4-String Patterns

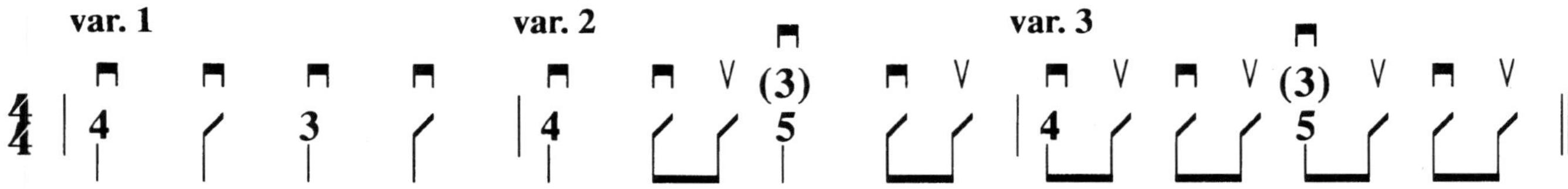

Here are a few alternating bass patterns that will work for tunes in 3/4 time. Notice that it takes two measures for the pattern to officially be an "alternating" bass pattern. For chords that only get one measure, simply play the first measure of each pattern.

6-String Patterns

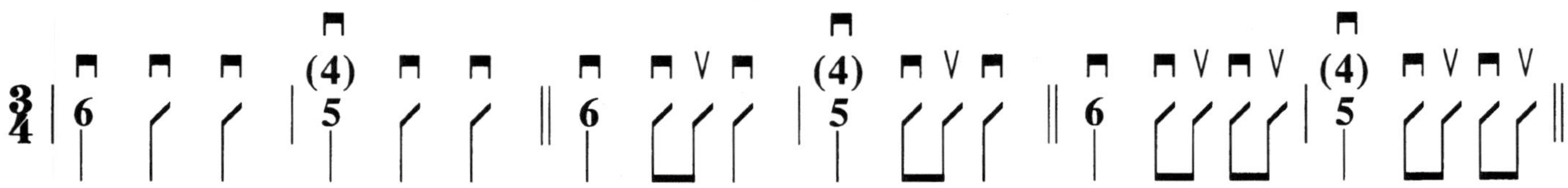

5-String Patterns

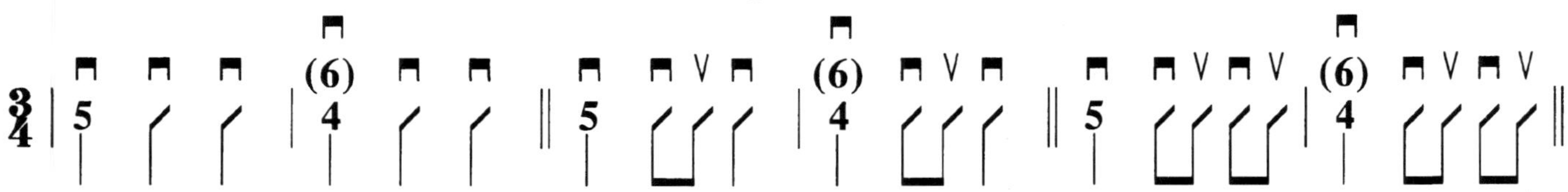

4-String Patterns

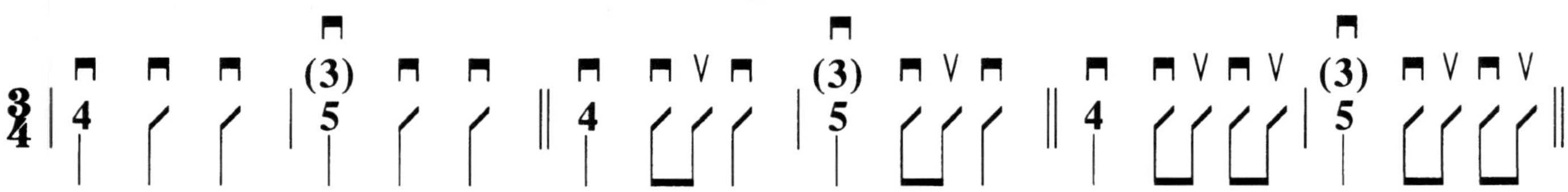

Use the following tunes and progressions to practice each alternating bass strum pattern. Feel free to put these patterns to use over any country or folk tune. Also, make up some original alternating bass strum patterns. Be sure to write them down so they may be remembered for future use.

Down in the Valley

27

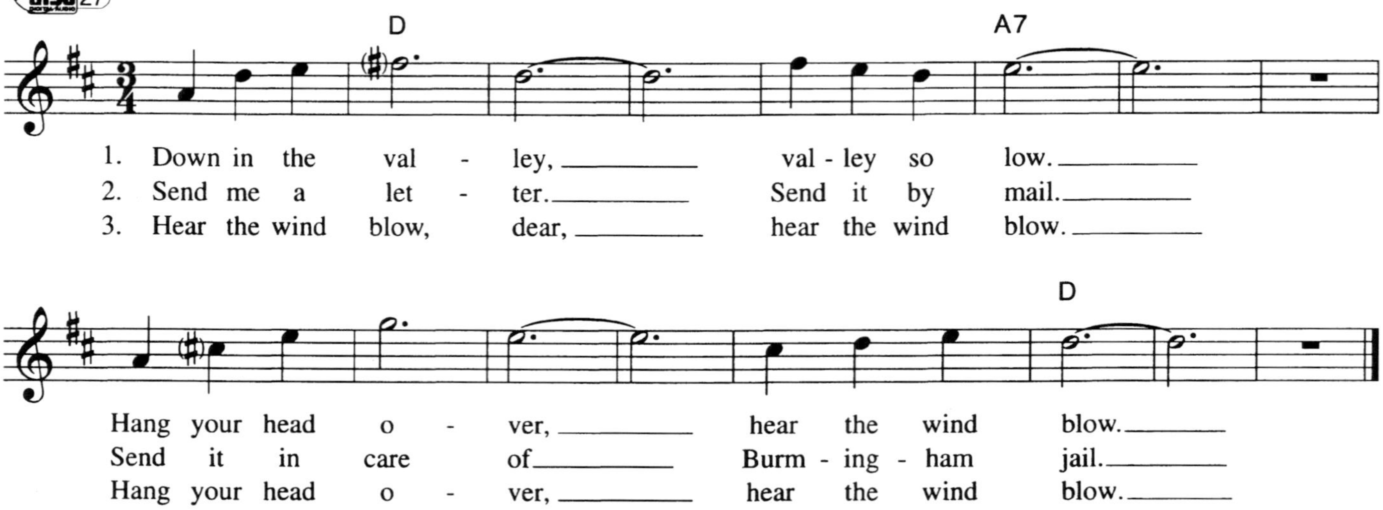

Going Down the Road Feeling Bad

28

Cripple Creek

Traditional

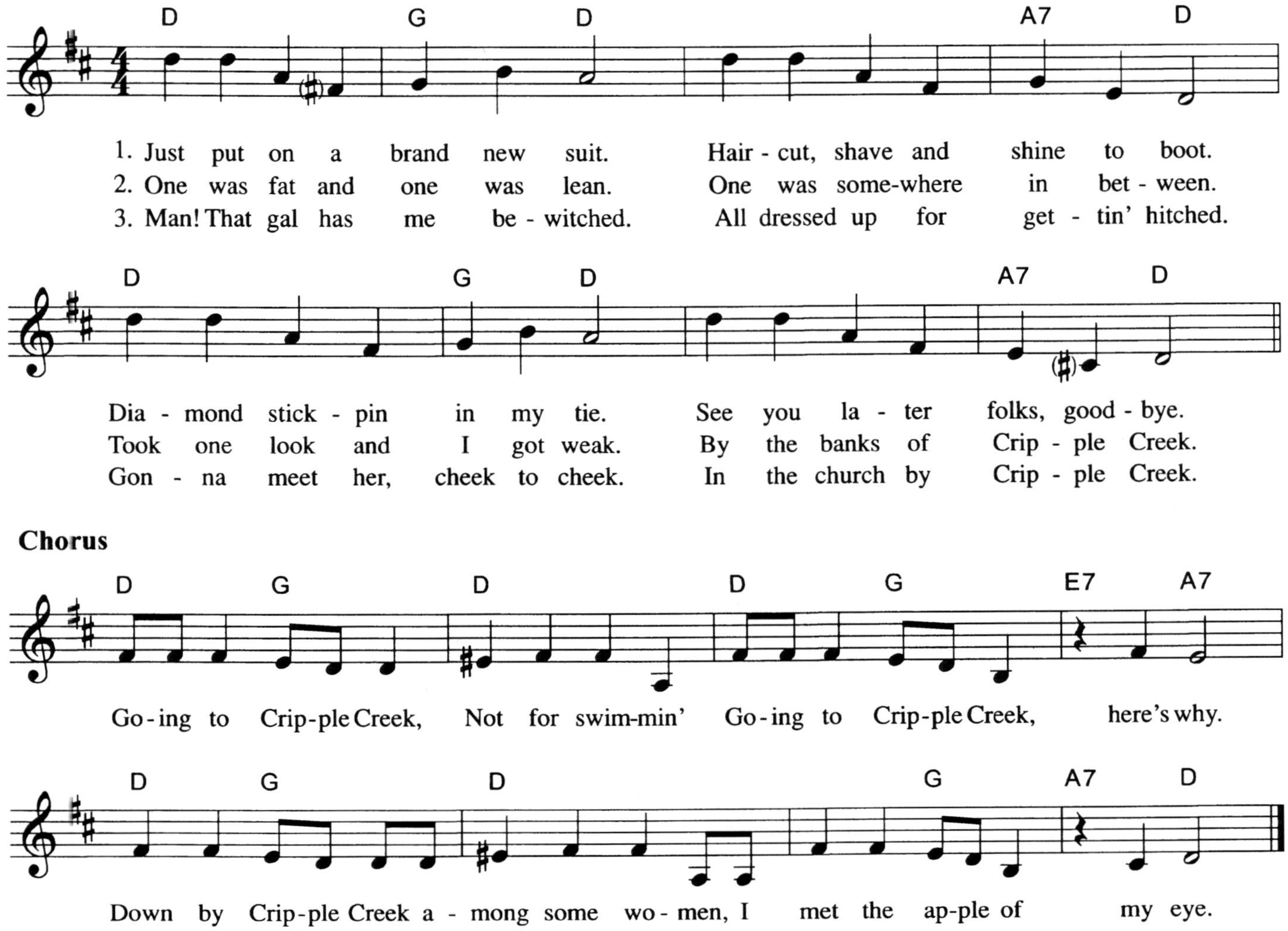

Fingerstyle Accompaniment

Fingerstyle accompaniment is a very important aspect of playing folk guitar. Country and folk guitar legends the likes of Merle Travis, Chet Atkins, James Taylor, and artists such as Robert Johnson and Rev. Gary Davis all have used fingerpicking patterns to give their guitar accompaniment a unique sound. The following fingerpicking patterns are to be applied to six-string, five-string, and four-string chords just as the alternating bass patterns. When applying these patterns, simply determine how many strings the chord being played uses and apply the pattern. When starting this type of accompaniment, it is suggested that one pattern (for each of the three chord types) be selected and played for the entire tune. After many patterns have been mastered, one can mix and match the patterns for a more spontaneous sound.

The following pattern will help guitarists coordinate the fingers of the right hand and prepare them for more involved patterns to follow.

① 4/4

	6-String Chords								5-String Chords								4-String Chords							
	6	2	4	3	6	2	4	3	5	2	4	3	5	2	4	3	4	1	3	2	4	1	3	2
Fingering:	*p*	*m*	*p*	*i*	*p*	*m*	*p*	*i*	*p*	*m*	*p*	*i*	*p*	*m*	*p*	*i*	*p*	*m*	*p*	*i*	*p*	*m*	*p*	*i*
Rhythm:	1	&	2	&	3	&	4	&	1	&	2	&	3	&	4	&	1	&	2	&	3	&	4	&

Disc 29

(Remember, right hand: *p* = thumb, *i* = index finger, *m* = middle finger, and *a* = ring finger. See page 7 and 8 for fingerstyle technique.)

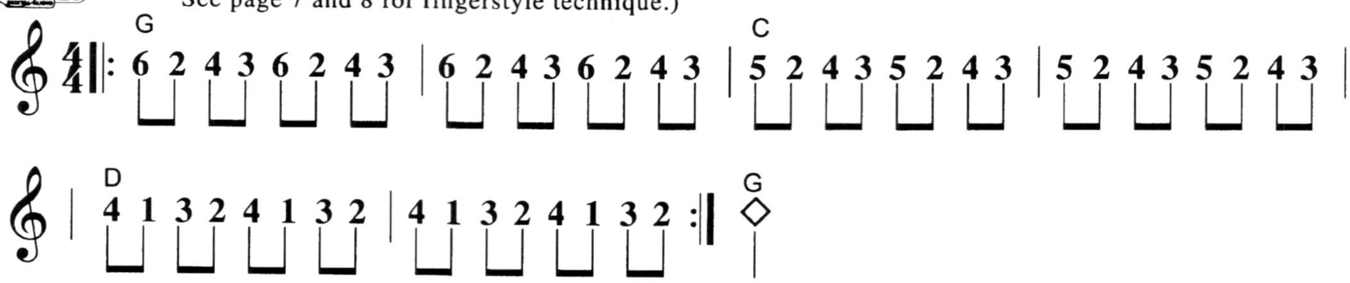

The next patterns work well over progressions and tunes in 4/4 and 3/4. Apply these patterns to the chord progressions below. Feel free to use different patterns over each of the chord progressions for practicing purposes. Also, use these patterns over any of the folk tunes in this book. The goal should be to apply all of the accompaniment patterns presented in a variety of ways and over a variety of tunes. Holding G, C, and D chords, practice each of the following fingerpicking patterns.

② 4/4 — Disc 30

6-String Chords								5-String Chords								4-String Chords							
6	–	4	3	6	2	4	3	5	–	4	3	5	2	4	3	4	–	3	2	4	1	3	2
p		*p*	*i*	*p*	*m*	*p*	*i*	*p*		*p*	*i*	*p*	*m*	*p*	*i*	*p*		*p*	*i*	*p*	*m*	*p*	*i*
1		2	&	3	&	4	&	1		2	&	3	&	4	&	1		2	&	3	&	4	&

③ 4/4 — Disc 31

6-String Chords								5-String Chords								4-String Chords							
6	4	3	2	6	4	3	2	5	4	3	2	5	4	3	2	4	3	2	1	4	3	2	1
p	*p*	*i*	*m*	*p*	*p*	*i*	*m*	*p*	*p*	*i*	*m*	*p*	*p*	*i*	*m*	*p*	*p*	*i*	*m*	*p*	*p*	*i*	*m*
1	&	2	&	3	&	4	&	1	&	2	&	3	&	4	&	1	&	2	&	3	&	4	&

④ 3/4 — Disc 32

6-String Chords						5-String Chords						4-String Chords					
6	4	3	2	4	3	5	4	3	2	4	3	4	3	2	1	3	2
p	*p*	*i*	*m*	*p*	*i*	*p*	*p*	*i*	*m*	*p*	*i*	*p*	*p*	*i*	*m*	*p*	*i*
1	&	2	&	3	&	1	&	2	&	3	&	1	&	2	&	3	&

NOTE: If two chords appear in a measure, divide the fingerpicking patterns and use the first part of each chord's pattern.

Two notes can be plucked simultaneously to add a rich, full sound to any of the above patterns. Here are a few examples of this technique. Try creating original patterns that make use of two notes being played at once. Remember to repeat the patterns making the appropriate adjustments for each of the three chord types. Many guitarists will use the high pitched extra note (when two notes are played at one time) to accentuate the melody of a tune. It is nice to play a melody note, when appropriate and playable, in the accompaniment.

⑤ 4/4 (stacked note over the first note)

	6-String Chords	5-String Chords	4-String Chords
Upper string	1	1	1
Strings	6 – 4 3 6 2 4 3	5 – 4 3 5 2 4 3	4 – 3 2 4 1 3 2
Upper finger	m	m	m
Fingers	p p i p m p i	p p i p m p i	p p i p m p i
Count	1 2 & 3 & 4 &	1 2 & 3 & 4 &	1 2 & 3 & 4 &

⑥ 4/4 (stacked note over the second note)

	6-String Chords	5-String Chords	4-String Chords
Upper string	1	1	1
Strings	6 – 4 – 6 2 4 3	5 – 4 – 5 2 4 3	4 – 3 – 4 1 3 2
Upper finger	m	m	m
Fingers	p p p m p i	p p p m p i	p p p m p i
Count	1 2 3 & 4 &	1 2 3 & 4 &	1 2 3 & 4 &

⑦ 4/4 (stacked note over the first note)

	6-String Chords	5-String Chords	4-String Chords
Upper string	1	1	1
Strings	6 4 3 2 6 4 3 2	5 4 3 2 5 4 3 2	4 3 2 1 4 3 2 1
Upper finger	m	m	m
Fingers	p p i m p p i m	p p i m p p i m	p p i m p p i m
Count	1 & 2 & 3 & 4 &	1 & 2 & 3 & 4 &	1 & 2 & 3 & 4 &

⑧ 4/4 (stacked notes over the third and seventh notes)

	6-String Chords	5-String Chords	4-String Chords
Upper string	2 2	2 2	1 1
Strings	6 4 3 4 6 4 3 4	5 4 3 4 5 4 3 4	4 3 2 3 4 3 2 4
Upper finger	m m	m m	m m
Fingers	p p i p p p i p	p p i p p p i p	p p i p p p i p
Count	1 & 2 & 3 & 4 &	1 & 2 & 3 & 4 &	1 & 2 & 3 & 4 &

⑨ 3/4 (stacked note over the first note)

	6-String Chords	5-String Chords	4-String Chords
Upper string	1	1	1
Strings	6 4 3 2 4 3	5 4 3 2 4 3	4 3 2 1 3 2
Upper finger	m	m	m
Fingers	p p i m p i	p p i m p i	p p i m p i
Count	1 & 2 & 3 &	1 & 2 & 3 &	1 & 2 & 3 &

⑩ 3/4 (stacked notes over the third and fifth notes)

	6-String Chords	5-String Chords	4-String Chords
Upper string	2 2	2 2	1 1
Strings	6 4 3 4 3 4	5 4 3 4 3 4	4 3 2 3 2 3
Upper finger	m m	m m	m m
Fingers	p p i p i p	p p i p i p	p p i p i p
Count	1 & 2 & 3 &	1 & 2 & 3 &	1 & 2 & 3 &

Use fingerpicking patterns to play the following tunes. (The CD recording demonstrates pattern 3 for *Shenandoah*, pattern 10 for *Scarborough Fair*, and Pattern 2 for *Worried Man Blues*.)

Shenandoah

Scarborough Fair

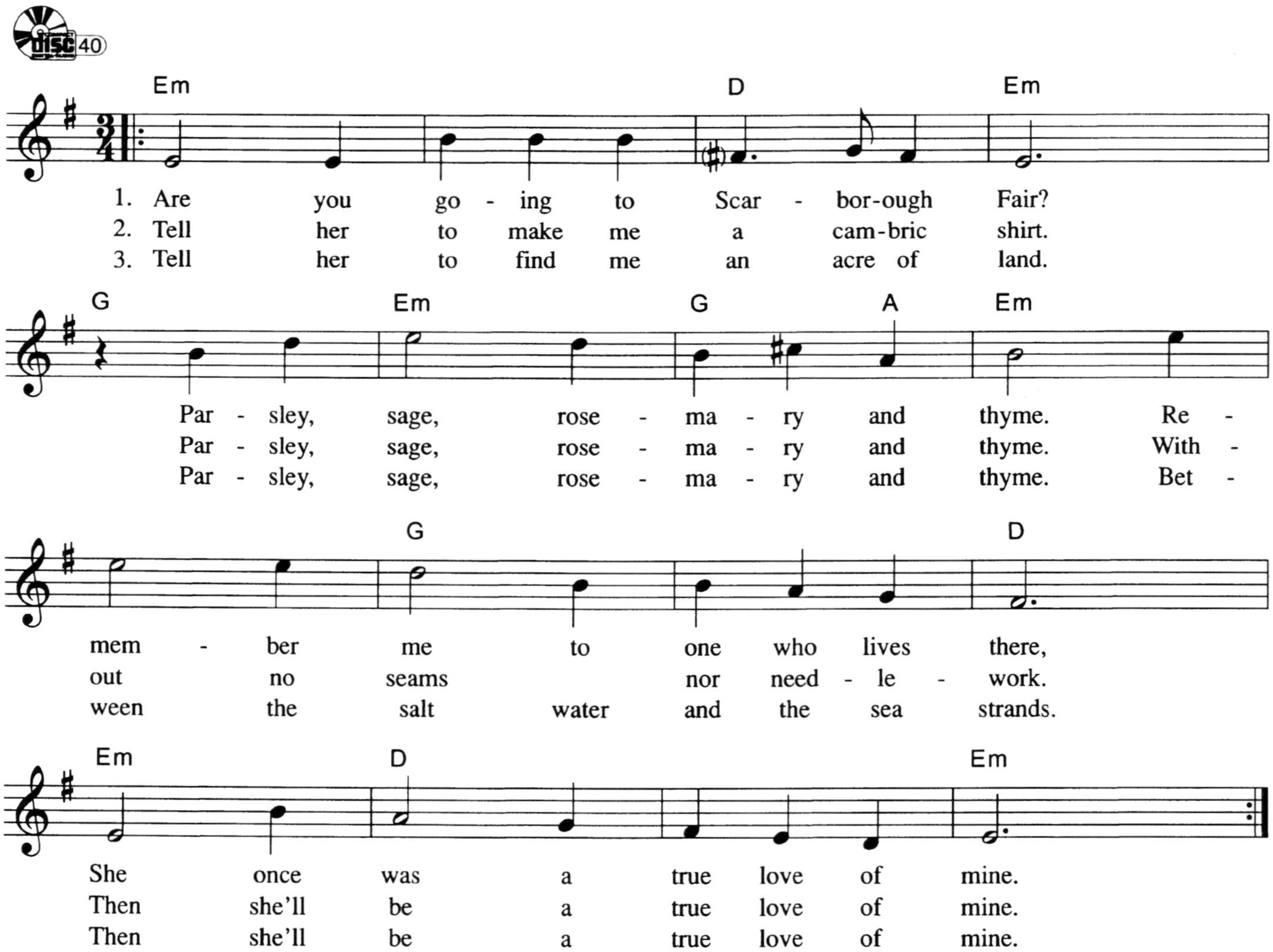

Worried Man Blues

Additional Verses:

2. I went across the river, and I lay down to sleep, (3 times)
   When I woke up, had shackles on my feet.
3. Twenty-nine links of chain around my leg, (3 times)
   And on each link, an initial of my name.
4. I asked that judge, tell me, what's gonna be my fine? (3 times)
   Twenty-one years on the Rocky Mountain Line.
5. Twenty-one years to pay my awful crime, (3 times)
   Twenty-one years — but I got ninety-nine.
6. The train arrived sixteen coaches long, (3 times)
   The girl I love is on that train and gone.
7. I looked down the track as far as I could see, (3 times)
   Little bitty hand was waving after me.
8. If anyone should ask you, who composed this song, (3 times)
   Tell him was I, and I sing it all day long.

MEL BAY®